The Karate Consciousness

THE
KARATE
CONSCIOUSNESS

From Worldly Warrior to Mystic Master

Founder & Grandmaster
Kiado-Ryu Martial Arts
The Karate Institute of America

RICHARD ANDREW KING

Richard Andrew King

© by Richard Andrew King
Published by Richard King Publications
PO Box 3621
Laguna Hills, CA 92654

Library of Congress Cataloging-in-Publication Data

King, Richard Andrew
The Karate Consciousness
    From Worldly Warrior to Mystic Master
Second Edition
ISBN: 978-0-931872-19-8

Richard King Publications

Date of Publication: 26 June 2017

ACKNOWLEDGEMENTS

My deepest appreciation to Chip "Hawk" Robinson
for his continuing support and friendship and whose
encouragement was primarily instrumental in the
publishing of this Second Edition.

A special thanks to Adam "Frog" Mahan for his
dedication to the Karate Institute of America
and his artistic book cover design talents.

Richard Andrew King

6

The "Black Belt World" logo pictured here is a trademark of Richard Andrew King and Kiado-Ryu Martial Arts. All rights reserved.

CONTACT

Richard Andrew King

PO Box 3621 Laguna Hills, CA 92654-3621

RichardKing.net | Kiado-Ryu.com | KingsKarate.net

THE KARATE CONSCIOUSNESS

From Worldly Warrior to Mystic Master

Table of Contents

#	Chapter	Page
	Author's Preface	9
1	Meanings	11
2	Power Precepts	25
3	The Continuum	45
4	Thought	77
5	Love	101
6	Individuality	125
7	Purity	141
8	The D.C. Factor	157
9	Strength	179
10	Priorities & Possessions	191
11	Teaching	207
12	Karma	223
13	Climbing The Mountain	233
	Index	247
	Richard Andrew King – Books	249
	Richard Andrew King – CDs	261
	Contact	263

Richard Andrew King

The Karate Consciousness

AUTHOR'S PREFACE

I began my martial arts journey in 1967 with the Tracy Brothers Kenpo Karate organization in San Jose, California, eventually reaching a 5th Dan Black Belt rating in their system. I also achieved a 1st Dan Black Belt rating in Ed Parker's Kenpo Karate system, having studied with their organization for a time.

Having fallen in love with martial arts, I opened my own studio – The Karate Institute of America – in Mission Viejo, CA, in 1979, and began developing the Kiado-Ryu System of Martial Arts. Defined, "Kiado-Ryu" means the family (Ryu) of the KIA (Karate Institute of America) way (Do). I have been teaching professionally ever since.

Throughout my fifty years of martial arts experience as both student and teacher, I have come to realize that it is one of the greatest vehicles for integrating the body, mind and spirit. Too, it offers an incredibly powerful opportunity for elevating one's consciousness to remarkable heights if one focuses not just on the fighting/mundane aspects of the art but also on the elevation and edification of the spirit and consciousness. Hence, the subtitle of this book: *From Worldly Warrior to Mystic Master.*

The gifts of martial arts training are endless. As I mention in *The Black Belt Book of Life – Secrets of a Martial Arts Master*, "Martial arts is life." No truer statement could be spoken.

Richard Andrew King

Everything in martial arts has a direct correlation with life itself. Aside from self-defense skills, here is a partial list of the life principles karate has to offer: balance, personal responsibility and accountability, reliability, individuality, humility, respect, strength, courage, confidence, will power, flexibility of body, mind and spirit; adaptability, discipline, control, concentration, creativity, patience, perseverance, persistence, determination, devotion, dedication, consistency, coordination, peace, love, practicality, movement, memorization, dignity, nobility, generosity, graciousness, gratitude, forgiveness and common sense.

Consciousness can be defined as the sum total of our knowledge, thought, understanding, awareness, perception, feeling and intuition. Basically, consciousness is the composite of who we are. Through martial arts dedication and training, we can expand our consciousness to areas never before imagined and touch levels of reality we never knew existed. The ideas, thoughts and concepts of this work are offered in the spirit of sharing what I have learned in my karate life in the hope that they may help other practitioners in advancing and expanding their consciousness of life. Verily, all of us who practice martial arts are infinitely blessed with a gift of enormous proportions. Let us not betray it but fully embrace it.

Yours in the Arts,
Richard Andrew King, Founder & Grandmaster
The Karate Institute of America & Kiado-Ryu Martial Arts
KingsKarate.net I Kiado-Ryu.com I RichardKing.net

The Karate Consciousness

Chapter I

MEANINGS

The true meaning of life is realized in the expression of Divine Perfection. It is the ultimate purpose of karate to assist the karateka in the fulfillment of this expression and to assist him in his transition from worldly warrior to mystic master. Therefore, the student is admonished:

Let your hands give wings to your mind
that you may find an ever-greater Power of Life,
a Power preserving the sanctity of your soul and
illuminating the radiance of your perfection.

Richard Andrew King

Karate means, "open hand." "Kara" signifying *open* and "te" signifying *hand*. In the preceding verse, "hands" in the first line symbolizes an individual's entire understanding of karate. "Wings" carries the meaning of flight, spiritual edification, elevation and upliftment. Thus, what the poem is saying is that the student should allow his complete understanding of karate to spiritually elevate his mind, i.e., consciousness, so that he may personally discover a power or powers of life greater in scope than mere animal prowess which karate, in its more mundane explanation, represents.

And, indeed, there are universal powers encompassing wider dimensions than karate can offer. A student of life will have some recollection, or will eventually gain it as his understanding increases, of supernatural powers exhibited by individuals who shall be referred to herein as Masters. These powers include mental telepathy, telekinesis, teleportation, the ability to disappear at will, the art of healing, walking on water, and feeding hundreds of people from a single loaf of bread.

However, all spiritual Masters warn against using such powers because their usage will inhibit the individual's inward and upward progress into higher realms of consciousness. In effect, such powers are traps for the individual and should be avoided. All spiritual power should be focused on the internal journey, not the external one.

Regarding supernatural powers, Saint Jagat Singh (20th Century) offers this warning from his book *The Science of the Soul.*

When one makes progress spiritually, marvelous powers come to him. One can heal the sick, cure the blind, cast out evil spirits, feed hundreds from one loaf of bread, walk on water, fly in the air and do a hundred thousand such miraculous acts. But there is nothing spiritual in it. This is the result only of a little concentration of the mind in the mental plane . . . But using these powers for personal ends is dangerous. It is playing into the hands of the Negative Power, Kal-the Satan.

To the current karate consciousness these powers probably lie somewhere between fiction and fairytale. But as man increases his understanding of the life force, he will come to know their veracity in time. Within the limitless boundary of infinity, he will gain an increasing awareness of the mystical nature of life, but in the interim he must have a means of developing his power at this level. Karate, as a developmental system, offers such a means.

PERSPECTIVE

To be correctly understood, karate must be placed in the proper perspective. Firstly, it should not be thought of as a panacea, a cure-all for the ills which plague an individual, such as an unconditioned body, mind or spirit; a lack of confidence; an

Richard Andrew King

inadequacy to protect oneself from aggression; a short supply of discipline; an absence of strength and so forth.

Karate may be regarded as a system of self-development but only one system applicable to a particular group of people. There are many avenues in which individuals can learn and grow as they move through the corridors of infinity. Karate offers one avenue. It is temporal, but it is a definite and viable method of personal development.

Secondly, karate shouldn't really be the center of a person's life. It is not God. It is a tool utilized to create or enhance the growth process of an individual. A student of the art will have to spend much time to learn it well but he should never forget that it is far more important to be a student of life first and a karateka second because karate is only one part of the whole. It is not the whole, and if an individual focuses too much and too long on it, considering it as the only part of his existence, he may be inhibiting the life-learning process and even running the risk of temporarily terminating his growth.

Another way of understanding this is to think of karate as a vehicle utilized to transport a person from one point in time and space to another. In this case, the first point may be a lack of discipline. The destination, or second point, may be the gaining of discipline and its subsequent expression in the individual. Karate can do the transporting. It can carry the student along the way of life for a specified distance but it cannot continue forever because it is a

The Karate Consciousness

system relegated to this level of creation. Therefore, it is finite. It has limitations and borders.

In learning to express discipline, karate may be the exact prescription for an individual. However, different people often need different prescriptions to cure an ill. Karate may not be the way to help one person but it may be the exact thing to assist another. Therefore, each person should choose the vehicle which best helps him in reaching his goals. Likewise, he should view karate from the standpoint of whether it will be beneficial for him as he pursues greater understandings and realities of life.

Ultimately, however, the student of life will have to disembark from his karate vehicle because, as opposed to this martial art, life – the true focus of an individual's learning – is infinite. It has no limitations, no boundaries, and there are lessons to be learned in life which render karate totally useless as far as assisting in the gaining of a solution or learning a particular lesson. It's like traveling from one place on planet earth to another as opposed to traveling to the moon. An automobile, plane or ship may expedite travel within the earth's environment but a different kind of vehicle is needed for interstellar transport, let alone mystical transport.

Thus, karate should be thought of as a tool, a vehicle, a system whereby the individual transports himself along the endless avenues of life. Karate is finite, temporary and, in view of the big picture, ephemeral. It is one part of the whole, an experience in

Richard Andrew King

passing, one stopover in the journey of infinity. This is one perspective of the art; a worthy perspective which each serious karateka should consider.

FOCUS

Spiritually speaking, in each person's journey through infinity his daily consideration should be to express more of his divinity today than he did the day before and to make plans for greater expression tomorrow. Thus, the tasks of the day are to learn and express. Each day there will be new lessons and, hopefully, a higher expression of the life force. Many of the lessons the author feels are important to the life-edification process are discussed later. They do not contain the complete list of such lessons, for could there ever be a complete list? If life is infinite, then will not its lessons also be infinite?

MASTERY

The term "Master" has been used previously. What, precisely, is a Master and what significance is there to the concept of mastery as it relates to karate?

In response to the first part of the preceding question, a Master is an individual who has learned to be "at one" with the life force, who has, indeed, mastered the lessons found within this plane of existence. It has been said that Jesus was a Master, as was Buddha.

The Karate Consciousness

These two distinguished expressions of divinity are more well known than others but there have been and will be others as well. Each individual is capable of mastery and of adorning the title "Master." Every great spiritual leader and teacher will corroborate this fact of man's existence.

What significance is there to the concept of mastery? Everything. Mastery is, "What it's all about," to use the vernacular. It is what karate is all about also because karate assists each person in learning to master himself and, thereby, to master the laws and principles of life relative to this level. If an individual is ever to express his divinity properly, if he is ever to live in and advance to higher plateaus of existence, if he is ever to be truly free – he must become a master of life, for it is in mastery that the beauty of life is fully recognized, experienced and appreciated. It is only through mastery of one task or level of existence that new tasks offering greater achievement, realization and experience can be obtained.

If each of us truly desires to grow and express life in fuller dimensions, then we must live in this concept of mastery. We must learn to master ourselves first and then proceed to other expressions of the life process. "God gave man dominion over all tings." But man, as a whole, hasn't functionally realized this truth. He lives in a state of non-mastery and, hence, suffers because of his inadequacy or state of non-realized and non-perfected ability.

This is no different from a child learning to walk or a person learning to drive a car. The child cannot walk and receive the benefits of such mobility until he has mastered the principles of balance, coordination and strength. An individual cannot reap the benefits of an automobile until he has mastered the procedures which make the vehicle operational. By the same token, a person cannot realize or receive the benefits which an enlightened consciousness offers until he has achieved a level of mastery commensurate with such realization. This is precisely why mastery is of such significance. Higher levels of existence cannot be achieved without it.

Because the mastery of life is of such preeminent importance, the karate consciousness must center itself in the study of life – not simply self-defense techniques or other expressions of animal prowess. To live and express life fully is the higher goal. The expression of death, violence, discord, disease, egotism, malevolence and other inimical attributes is not a true reason for studying karate, for if karate does not serve to uplift mankind, it serves no real purpose.

How does it uplift mankind? By helping those who study it to learn various lessons which will increase their own understanding of life, thereby adding more wisdom to the amount already in the pot, so to speak, i.e., the amount currently realized on planet earth, and, thus, raise the whole – at least by one individual consciousness. Of course, as history bears witness, a single person's uplifted consciousness can affect many minds positively, just as a lighted candle illuminates more darkness than an amount of space coincident with the size of its flame.

The Karate Consciousness

As stated in the opening paragraph of this book, the purpose of karate is to assist the student in fulfilling his expression of Divine Perfection, his at-one-ment with that universal force which created him, which creates and permeates all things, all time, and all space. An expression such as this can only be gained by a mastery of the principles of life. Such mastery is not an easy task but certainly an obligatory one if an individual is ever to express his divinity, or divine identity, as it is meant to be expressed.

For a more in-depth understanding of Masters, read *Messages from the Masters – Timeless Truths for Spiritual Seekers* available at RichardKing.net and major online book sellers and retailers.

CONTRARY BELIEFS

There are those beliefs in the karate world today that deprecate and deny any thought which does not coincide with animal warfare or the development of animal skills. Some individuals only believe that karate was meant for fighting. In fact, this belief is ostensibly the belief of the majority. In one way or another most people associate karate with some sort of combat, offensive or defensive, while totally overlooking, disregarding or not recognizing its more meaningful associations and attributes. It must be remembered, too, that the current karate consciousness of the majority is the combination of individual consciousnesses, that in order to change the whole each part of the whole must be altered.

Richard Andrew King

The karate consciousness of today, as a whole, would be benefited if it were edified. In too many circles, by too many people in too many places, karate is regarded solely in combative terms, in the jargon of warfare and fighting. But as the saying goes, "Those who live by the sword, die by the sword," and, consequently, those who dwell in the thought of combat and violence experience the same.

But the reverse is also true – those who live in the thought of life, peace, harmony, love and understanding experience their qualities. It is a grave injustice to contribute to the perpetuation of violent or combative beliefs, especially when they affect the whole as they do. This is why the karate consciousness would benefit mankind if it were elevated. It would serve the student with true meaning, with a purpose focused on edification, spiritual growth, enlightenment and understanding. Such a task is left to those sentient individuals whose percipience will give greater impetus to truth and the required alterations.

THE IRONY

Karate, mundanely defined, is basically an animalistic art. It is primitive, physical, the epitome of bestial prowess. Yet, its higher purpose is to elevate the student above such beastliness, not promote it. Hopefully, in the study of karate, an individual will come to recognize that it is quite mundane, earthly. Although it can be utilized to enhance spiritual development to a point, in and of itself it is not traditionally reflective of a truly ethereal way of life.

Man's highest law is love. Yet, karate pits one man against another. It presupposes discord and hostility and, therefore, is predicated on some form of combat – either defensive or offensive. In love, however, there is no combative violence. There is no need to pit one person – a divine creation, against any other. If all people expressed a functional understanding of love in its truest form, karate would have no existence.

Earthly man, however, has not reached such divine states of consciousness. Therefore, karate exists. It is an expression of his beastliness, not his ethereality. But it can be efficacious in the edification process if utilized correctly. And the correct usage of karate is where the battle lies in today's world because karate is greatly abused, misused, misunderstood or not understood at all in relation to its higher meaning, which is, of course, to assist the student in the expression of his divine perfection.

BEASTLY VERSUS ETHEREAL

"Beastly" pertains to that which is animalistic, primitive, mundane. If one man wants to go out and fight another, such action is beastly – of and pertaining to beasts. Animals fight. They do so because, lacking in intellect, they know of no other way to solve problems. Physical combat is generally all they know.

Richard Andrew King

When man resorts to physical violence to solve problems, he is expressing traits which are animalistic. Yet, man has intellect, and the higher laws of life require its use. If and when man does not use his intellect to solve problems but resorts to beastly behavior, he is lowering his status as an expression of the life force. He is deprecating, depreciating his own being, and such self-degradation does not speak well for his level of development and attainment.

It is naturally characteristic for animals to fight; quite the contrary with man's higher ideal. Yet, in the karate world of today, the emphasis is on fighting, hence, beastliness, and such concepts result in man expressing a lower ideal than is established in his true identity. The conclusion here is that the karate consciousness of the contemporary world is, by and large, animalistic. It is in dire need of an overhaul and an uplift.

"Ethereal" pertains to that which is celestial, heavenly. This is man's true nature. It requires the use of intellect and mental prowess, as opposed to animal prowess. Ethereality is, by its own definition, a higher expression than beastliness.

An ethereal consciousness is marked by love, harmony, peace, intellect, health, discipline, strength, wisdom and understanding – all of these attributes being functional, not merely academic.

As each student increases his expression of these celestial characteristics, his own consciousness, as well as the general level of the mass consciousness, will be raised. He will become a higher and, indeed, greater expression of the life force and also help karate to reflect the same greatness.

The karate consciousness of the old thought is outdated. But the new consciousness, hopefully the one which is dawning, will one day come fully into its own. It is a consciousness centered in and expressive of ever-increasing dimensions of enlightenment, and one in which each student of the art is continually elevated in the understanding of his Divine Perfection.

Richard Andrew King

The Karate Consciousness

Chapter 2

POWER PRECEPTS

Man was not created to dominate his fellow man. He was created to live in the fullness of the Light and to radiate that Light throughout the corridors of the universe.

The karate consciousness of today is not centered in the fullness of the Light – divine illumination and understanding as characterized by life, love, peace, perfection, purity, prosperity, health, harmony, strength and wisdom. Rather, and quite noticeably, it is centered in a consciousness of dominance and what shall be referred to herein as the *Power in the Flock Syndrome*.

Richard Andrew King

POWER

For purposes of discussion, this chapter concerns itself with two specific kinds of power: *intrinsic* and *extrinsic*. The former is the ideal, the goal of all serious karatekas who choose to follow the ascending path of the mystical master. The latter, *extrinsic power*, is anathematic. It is inimical to the well-being of the student and his growth because it ties and binds his mind to a worldly focus only and, therefore, should be avoided if a higher consciousness is to be achieved.

Intrinsic power is true power. It originates from *within* the individual being, and there is only one way to tap it and that is to go *within* and seek it. Once found, it can be brought forth and utilized to increase the student's functional understanding and expression of life.

Intrinsic power, sometimes referred to as *internal* power, is the only force which can lead to self-mastery. Thus, it needs to be cultivated and cared for as a farmer cares for and cultivates his crops.

The source of this power is the Creator of all things. This "Creator" is often referred to as God, the Great White Father, the Father Within, etc. The label attached to this omnipresent, omniscient and omnipotent force is not as important as knowing that it exists. It is real. It is.

The Karate Consciousness

In order to generate intrinsic power the student must begin by realizing that it is not so much created as it is tapped into and subsequently utilized by the individual. It already exists. It simply needs to be brought forth.

The technique of "bringing forth" this power is to align oneself with the Creator of all things, its supreme intelligence and force. Karate serves the student in helping him to effectuate this alignment so he can manifest this power from within his own being and move forward toward a state of self-mastery.

This is, most assuredly, not an easy task even when consciously realized. Bringing forth this power requires labor – mental, spiritual and physical work. But when viewed in the proper perspective it is a labor of love and its results are pure artistry.

Intrinsic power is free for all men. It cannot be purchased, sold or traded. Nor can it be hoarded as a miser hoards his money. It must be used to be realized. If it is not used, the concept of it dissipates from the consciousness and it, therefore, slips into a status of non-realization. It still remains a universal fact, but if man does not utilize it, he cannot realize or acknowledge it as a part of his being.

As a student learns to bring forth this power from within the depths of his own soul, he becomes one with the power. In that oneness he realizes true freedom. He becomes strong, solid, not because he, in his finite self, is powerful, but because he has allowed the power from his Creator to flow through him and, thus,

Richard Andrew King

empower him, just as electricity flowing through a magnet empowers it.

Students who desire to express mastery must, therefore, learn to become channels for this flow of divine power. This is a great art. It is the way to true accomplishment, and it is the only way to divine self-realization.

THE COIN REVERSED

Extrinsic power, on the other hand, is totally different. It is not true power because it cannot exist without the corroborative support of other people. In other words, it needs other individuals to take form. Extrinsic power can't exist by itself because it is nothing. It may appear to have substance but, like a mirage, it is only an illusion which vanishes with the onset of a discerning mind.

Unlike intrinsic power, the extrinsic form is totally separate from the individual being. It does not come from within but exists in the without – hence, extrinsic. The individual doesn't need it for vertical growth. In fact, becoming adept in the usage of extrinsic power can markedly inhibit and even halt the growth process. The student should learn to recognize it only so he can avoid it. It is this kind of power which is the basis of the *Power in the Flock Syndrome* and, as implied, this syndrome is antithetical to the student's well-being.

The Karate Consciousness

To elucidate further, extrinsic power exists only when one individual or individuals dominate or are dominated by another or others. He who claims power only when he can render another person subservient really has no power, at least not the kind which is meaningful. Remove all individuals capable of being dominated or manipulated from his environment and he becomes powerless.

An individual who manifests intrinsic power may also appear to be dominant. However, the difference lies in the manner in which the power is used. He who uses the extrinsic form seeks only to dominate, control and make subservient another while he who is intrinsically powerful seeks only personal growth and enlightenment for all. He has no need to dominate and control others in order to realize power because he is, indeed, already powerful. For others he desires only that they realize the power within themselves, as he realizes the same power within himself.

Extrinsic power is a denotation of a lack of security, intellect or love. Knowing that he is void of true power, the extrinsically oriented individual tries to achieve it by being imperious. The power he really seeks, however, is not to be found without. It lies within his own divine being, and the obvious solution for him is to begin exploring the depths of his own soul. He can never be free as long as he utilizes extrinsic power because the forces he uses to dominate others will dominate him. As his bread is "cast upon the water," so his concepts and actions of dominance will return to chain him to the ground, strengthening the shackles of his captivity.

Richard Andrew King

THE POWER IN THE FLOCK SYNDROME DEPICTED

To give greater understanding to this concept of extrinsic power let us use the following examples.

First, the training of a karateka involves many aspects, one of which is controlled combat or sparring. The technical term is "kumite" (pronounced *koo muh tey*). This is done to facilitate the development of control, poise, execution of movement, focus and so forth. It should always be done in an atmosphere of respect and concern for the sparring partner with the goal of learning held in paramount position. It should not be an exercise in which are expressed vibrations of hate, revenge, malevolence or dominance. Yet, such is the case in many instances. This is especially true of karate tournaments where many aspiring martial artists come to prove their physical ability to accentuate their power in the flock. They attend the social combative festivities to prove one thing generally – their ability to dominate all others. In the karate world of today the trend is to physically knock out the opponent. Such are the machinations of extrinsic power.

It is questionable whether these events are in the highest good of the student. Even if there is no malevolence among opponents, there still exists the condition of extrinsic power and the dominance theme, which is contrary to man's higher ideals. Man, however, should not be so disposed. He needs to grow out of his propensity toward animal prowess because he is greater than such manifestations. But as long as he sows the seeds of such concepts, he shall reap them. That is the universal law.

To reiterate, the purpose of karate is not to perpetuate animal prowess and promote personal, evolutionary stagnation, but to assist each individual in the fulfillment of his Divine Perfection. To promote divinity, not animal personality; to elevate, not degrade; to enlighten, not darken – this is the true purpose of karate, the goal of sentient karatekas and serious martial artists.

The Power in the Flock Syndrome manifests itself in other ways than simply through physical prowess. In situations of material wealth, prestige or position where a substantial level of enlightenment is scarce or absent, it is quite prevalent.

For example, a salesman has an appointment to give a sales presentation of his product to a customer. The salesman arrives in time for the appointment and is told to wait for a few minutes. Finally, when gaining entrance to his customer's office, the customer, trying to exercise dominance, as if it were really needed, carries on the entirety of the conversation sitting with his back to the salesman. This is one variation of the non-recognition technique for obtaining power in the flock. If the customer were intrinsically powerful, as he is in his rightful state, he wouldn't have to engage in such menial behavior. However, because he lacks in personal security, intellect or love, he does. Thus, he perpetuates the flock-power syndrome.

Richard Andrew King

Another example. The manager of a retail store arrives at work one morning. His assistant managers have already arrived and are sitting together at a table. He would like to speak to them. However, rather than join his assistants where they are sitting, he motions them to another table where he conducts his business. He does this for no other reason than to exercise his degree of power in the flock. His actions say, "I am boss. I direct. You follow." This is a dominance technique, an expression of extrinsic power.

The flock-power syndrome is not in keeping with man's highest good. Perhaps, however, there may be times when it is justified because in order for it to be non-existent there must be enlightenment on both sides. All people must share a mutual respect for each other. All must do their work and perform to the best of their ability.

To create harmonious conditions there must be reciprocity. If, in the above example, the manager joined his assistants where they were sitting, the latter should still recognize his position and responsibility and acknowledge it rather than undermine it by thinking of him as "just one of the boys." If the manager took this action, they should see it as a non-expression of the flock-power syndrome and reciprocate by not playing power games, i.e., not allowing their familiarity with the manager to hinder their work performance.

From the higher point of view, if the manager exhibits a large degree of intrinsic power, his position of responsibility cannot be

The Karate Consciousness

undermined by any action. However, in an elevated state of affairs there would never be any reason to discuss such circumstances anyway. Each person would understand his role in the business, be it leader or follower, and do it while respecting everyone else and the job they must do, whether it is mopping floors or managing the entire operation. Simply because one individual may have more responsibility than another does not preclude nor obviate the principle of man's inherent and divine state of equality.

The following statement will always be valid: *Intrinsic power will obviate extrinsic power every time.* It will do so because the former lies in a higher state of consciousness than is obtainable by the latter. Whereas an individual desiring to be externally powerful will attempt to play power games, the one who is internally powerful will not. He is an expression of individual solidarity and integration, while the other is an expression of individual non-solidarity and disintegration. One is whole; the other, incomplete.

It is this concept of disintegration and incompleteness which creates the Power in the Flock Syndrome. Because an individual has not realized his wholeness nor expressed a functional level of intrinsic power, he consciously or unconsciously feels weakness and tries to overcome it, which is the right thing to do from a developmental standpoint. However, he often does so by using other people to create it. If he can get someone to act in accordance with his will, either by position, money, deceit, physical prowess or obtrusiveness, he feels powerful. He's made someone move. But his power is extrinsic. What he fails to realize is that the person who moved in accordance with his will may not always be around to create his power. When the person is gone, the power is gone and he's back to the starting point – how to acquire true power and express personal integration, completeness, solidarity.

THE RADIANT IMAGE

In order to gain intrinsic power the student must begin with the correct concept of himself and all mankind. This concept is that, in his true form, each individual is a beautiful, resplendent and magnificently unique expression of the life force. He is one of the most powerful ideas in all of the universe because it is through him that divine intelligence is expressed and given form. He is the manifestation of the great dynamic "I AM," the hallmark of spiritual illumination. He is one grand, majestic, indivisible whole – a complete, harmonious expression of divine principle.

Each person is, by design, separate from other entities. He possesses his own identity and, therefore, there is absolutely no need for him to relinquish or subordinate himself to another. He is by divine right free, autonomous and sovereign.

In his spiritually enlightened form man is perfect, for he was created in the image and likeness of perfection, not imperfection. His true image is the manifestation of life, light and love. It is unassailable, it is impregnable, it radiates illumination, and it edifies and inspires all living things.

Man is master of life and destiny. He has only to act upon this truth to corroborate its validity. He is, to be sure, a creator, and he has only to monitor the effects of his thoughts and actions to realize this fact of his existence.

Man is separate, unique, distinct. When the student functionally realizes that these traits are part of his divinity, or divine identity, he will be well on the way to higher levels of enlightenment. With this understanding he will become more intrinsically powerful because it is this kind of understanding which assists him in consciously realizing his atonement, or at-one-ment, the place from which divine power flows.

As man lives in the fullness of this power, he realizes that it is *through* him that the great deeds of the earth are accomplished. It is *through* him that other people are uplifted and motivated. It is *through* him that the whole world is prospered. It is *through* him that all people are loved – not *because* of him but *through* him.

By natural right man is heir to the rich kingdom of divine creation. He is wealthy, healthy, holy, harmonious, pure and perfect – the manifestation of living light and love. He is beautiful. He is effulgent. He is free.

Richard Andrew King

As the student sees himself in this manner, he must learn to see all men in the same way. As he is a creation of divine principle, so they are a creation of divine principle. As he is divinely perfect, so they are divinely perfect. As he is whole, so they are whole. As he is free, so they are free. As he is unique and individually separate, so they are likewise.

Arriving at this understanding, the student will realize he has no need to dominate anyone else, nor will he possess any desire to do so. Because he sees freedom in all people, he does not want to suppress it but allow it greater expression. He doesn't need someone else to realize a feeling of power. He is power.

Thus, having started with the correct understanding of himself and those around him, the student will make noticeable progress in his personal development. He will be an expression of intrinsic power, not extrinsic power, and relegate any expression of the Power in the Flock Syndrome to the isles of oblivion where it belongs and thus move forward and upward into the glorious splendor of the Light.

> A helping hand,
> A sincere smile,
> An appreciative understanding
> May win a man's love,
> But what will be gained
> Through his defeat?

The Karate Consciousness

THE MYTH

Karate has often been used as a tool for the promotion of flock power. That this is the main purpose of karate is a myth, a false belief. Karate exists to promote life, to help the student along in his growth until he can move on and beyond to greater plateaus of existence.

The karate consciousness of today is centered in the Power in the Flock Syndrome. Movies, magazines and books have exploited the more violent interpretations of the art. The more popular belief is practically the reverse of what it should be. Life, not death; love, not hate; peace, not violence; spiritual growth, not manifestations of extrinsic power – these are the more meaningful concepts which should be emulated.

Another facet of the myth is the propensity toward fighting, the expression of animal prowess and consciousness. It would seem that physical combat and karate go hand-in-hand because when most people think of the art they regard it in combative terms. This is the substance of the mass consciousness. And this is not to say that such an observation is incorrect. In today's world it is, indeed, valid, sadly.

The higher interpretation, however, would be for karate to be instantly associated with personal growth and development. For this to occur the karate world will have to elevate its own

Richard Andrew King

functional concept of itself. This means that it must have a large number of its students, and preferably a majority, actively centered in studying karate for its more ethereal contributions, not its animal manifestations. Such a cause not only requires enlightenment but courage. Students must be willing to say, "No," to the constant perpetuation of fighting skills and take an unequivocal stand for higher learning and its manifestation.

What good is fighting anyway? What long term, positive good has ever occurred as the result of destructive combat? What problems have been definitely solved through warfare? Our world has temporarily solved some of its disagreements through warfare, but what has this led to except a civilization of paranoid power groups who, for fear of their lives and ideologies, have amassed systems of weaponry capable of annihilating the human race. Is this a positive good? Is this a reflection of beauty, peace, harmony, love?

The preceding passage deals with the macro, the big picture. But the same is also true of the micro, the smaller parts which combine to form the whole. Karate is part of the whole and it mirrors it as well. If a man will use the animal skills of karate to solve a problem, i.e., if he will engage in needless physical combat, he will probably also use nuclear weaponry in a like manner. The only difference between hand-to-hand combat and atomic energy is the sophistication and degree of fire power. The principles are the same. A problem arises and it is solved with fighting. This is the way of the unenlightened flock, the seekers of extrinsic power.

The Karate Consciousness

One of the most inimical conditions of utilizing animal combat to solve problems, which generally goes unnoticed, is the relationship of effect to cause. If it is true that every action has an equal and opposite reaction and that every cause has an effect, it is worth considering that any action involving violence, malevolence, animosity, etc., will generate a like effect in the opposite direction.

For example: if an individual maliciously inflicts bodily damage on another, or even mental suffering, he will, through the operation of this law of cause and effect, receive a commensurate amount of suffering. This is not a pleasant thing to think about but as a truth it should certainly warrant consideration from the student. In other words, if a person hurts someone else, he is going to be hurt somehow, sometime, some place, pursuant to the law of cause and effect. But by the same token, if an individual creates only actions of love, peace, harmony, etc., he will, in effect, cause the same conditions to be manifested in his experience. The student should, therefore, be made to understand that if he fights unjustifiably he will bring upon himself the results of such action.

From the foregoing argument it should be relatively clear that fighting is not an intelligent endeavor to engage in. He who fights and lives in the consciousness of animal combat – mental or physical – will only create non-edifying conditions in his experiences. In such a situation he will never be free but will remain trapped in a mire of animal consciousness and suffer from all the manifestations thereof.

Richard Andrew King

The student, therefore, is strongly admonished to consider his desire to learn karate strictly for its combative techniques. He is exhorted to center his studies on growth, self-development, and the expressions of ethereality as exemplified by life, love, peace, prosperity, harmony, truth, understanding, wisdom, health, holiness and enlightenment. This is the basis for obtaining higher levels of consciousness – the end result of all learning. And it is, too, the beginning of the end of the myth of karate being merely a tool for the perpetuation of power in the flock.

This is not to say that karate skills and knowledge should not be used to protect oneself from harm. They should be used where appropriate. The germane point is that karate power shouldn't be utilized to the exclusion of higher truths and behaviors. Use karate power where appropriate – to defend yourself – but not to expand your ego to the point of egocentricity and abusive flock power.

There exists another false belief within the structure of the contemporary karate consciousness. It is the theory of man versus man; that each individual must compare himself to another and be better than the other.

This generally takes form in the arena, the habitat for the seekers of extrinsic power. In order to substantiate who is the better fighter the individuals enter the ring to spar, i.e., fight. The victor emerges clothed in the garments of animal prowess and temporal self-satisfaction. But, unbeknownst to him, he remains trapped in the dungeon of darkness, a slave to his mortal propensities.

The Karate Consciousness

Why does the thought of one individual being better than another have to exist? Man does not have to compare himself with other men in such a manner. It is not important who is better than whom. It is only important for each person to seek the Light and live in the fullness of its radiation. It is far more ethereal for one person to love another, to be actively concerned about his well-being, his freedom, his functional enlightenment than it is to subordinate himself to another's will. As people, we should not live to compare. We should live simply to enjoy the experience of living and being.

Too, trying to be better than another individual can be a limiting thought. In the first place it detracts the person from living in and appreciating his own identity. No man or woman can be another. Each is himself, as basic as this may seem, and each must learn to accept himself individually and function individually, not as others would accept him or expect him to function.

This idea is referred to by psychologists and educators as peer pressure – doing what the group (flock) wants to do regardless of its effect on the individual.

For example, a group of individuals desire to commit a crime. One member of the group doesn't want to participate. However, in order to fulfill the desire of the group, he goes along with them. Such an action is obviously a result of peer pressure because if the person had been individually isolated from the group or personally stronger, his actions would have been different. He would not have

Richard Andrew King

succumbed to the desire of the flock and in so doing would have maintained his personal identity, avoiding criminal activity and its negative effects of prosecution and possible incarceration.

Peer pressure is flock pressure. The student must learn to recognize it and, if need be, guard against it. He can do this by isolating himself from the flock or having enough strength of character to nullify its pressure. He must know that because he is an individual he has free will – the ability to choose for himself, and he also has the prerogative to exercise it as he wishes.

The group may not always be right. In fact, a group decision may be quite antithetical and deleterious to any person in it. Therefore, the student must be prepared to sequester himself from it. Personal integrity is more important than popularity or likeability.

In such a separation the student will obviously stand alone. And if there is to be greater enlightenment in the karate world, it will take individuals who can see the light to stand alone, to be separate, to express their opinion by such actions and, therefore, effectuate some salutary changes in the mass consciousness.

As 19th Century Norwegian playwright, theater director, and poet Henrik Ibsen so powerfully acknowledged:

The strongest man in the world is he who stands most alone.

The Karate Consciousness

Perhaps one of the only instances in which one student should compare himself with another is contrasting his own degree of enlightenment and understanding with another. If someone else's is higher, the student should consider discovering why it is so and emulate, not the individual, but the ideal he expresses. Thus, the student will be benefited and his growth enhanced.

As he learns from one person, the student will eventually discover that all people are his teachers. Each individual has something to offer which will be of value to the student's developmental process. And, when he begins to learn from all people, he will not want to dominate any of them because dominance suppresses, and in a state of suppression man is not free to live, breathe, create and share experiences, which would be beneficial to all men.

The enlightened student will never seek to dominate. Even if he perceives a weakness in an individual which would allow that individual to be dominated, he avoids the utilization of extrinsic power. Regarding a weak or insecure person, intrinsically powerful individuals will strive to strengthen that weakness because they know that as long as it exists the entire race is hampered, its growth stunted. Never dominance of any but enlightenment for all – this is the consciousness which edifies and assists all men in the quest to realize their divine heritage.

Richard Andrew King

IN CONCLUSION

The karate consciousness of today needs to be edified, uplifted. Students should center their lessons in enlightenment and avoid this deleterious nectar, this psychic potion called extrinsic power. They must learn to live in the fullness of their own divinity and express that divinity in such a manner that it reaches out and helps all mankind. They must extricate themselves from the Power in the Flock Syndrome – that pattern of thought which attempts to dominate in order to realize completeness, and, contrastingly, seek that intrinsic power which flows from within. In doing this they will assist in raising the karate consciousness to a level where it is expressive of love, life and light – the garments of immortality – and they, in manifesting such enlightenment, will move forever higher in their own consciousness as they traverse the unchartered frontiers of infinity.

Chapter 3

THE CONTINUUM

Out of the bonds of mortal thought,

Away from the gravity of earth,

Man may relinquish the chains of his mind

And fly through the universe.

He may soar, and glide and ride

The waves of a boundless sea,

Bathing in the splendor of crystalline light

And the consciousness of infinity.

And as he traverses this endless space,

This timeless realm where he is free,

His soul will acquire the raiment of the Son

And the garments of his immortality.

Richard Andrew King

As surely as man, when viewed in the proper perspective, is divine, so life, when perceived in the fullness of its dimensions, is infinite. To be sure, life is a continuum – an endless sequence of experience.

This earth, this plane of existence, is an institution of learning, a school which serves to promote individual growth and development by offering a multifarious array of educational opportunities. The curriculum is expansive and not all courses are conducive to the student's well-being. When selecting courses of study, prudence must be exercised, for the goal is, after all, to challenge specific subjects of study, master them, graduate and ascend to higher levels of learning.

Karate is one course offered in the curriculum at this level. Of itself it is not a prerequisite for higher learning but, as mentioned previously, it may be utilized as a vehicle to transport the student across or through that territory in which lessons required for advancement can be learned. That "territory" is the space between worldly warriorship and mystical mastery.

EXPANSION

As the student expands his concept of karate and its more meaningful purpose of assisting in the individual expression of divine perfection, he should also begin to expand his understanding of life, for it is only in this expansion that he will break the bonds of his captivity and realize his inherent freedom.

This expansion of the life consciousness is an ineluctable task if the student is ever to realize his divinity, i.e., it cannot be avoided. It must be tackled with a fervent desire and indomitable spirit because it is not something that can be received as a gift is received by one person from another. It must be earned.

In beginning this "consciousness expansion" the individual may begin by scrutinizing his own understanding of life. Is it finite? That is to say, is life characterized by definite boundaries and a limited existence? Or is it infinite, characterized by absolutely no boundaries whatsoever and an illimitable existence?

In trying to answer this question the student could consult many texts, many people, many schools of thought both past and present. Such activities, however, are not necessary. In order to perceive the correct answer to his life's time span, be it finite or infinite, he simply needs to consult with one source – the center of his own Being. It is there he will find the answer to almost anything, if not everything, for his soul is forever united with its source, the Creator of all things. When this question is asked sincerely and the student listens sincerely, he will receive his own answer, but there is only one answer. It is applicable to all men and it is the truth of our existence.

Richard Andrew King

In helping to discover the answer to this question these thoughts are given: Is it easier to conceive of an existence which is encased by definite boundaries or one which is unequivocally free of all obstruction? Which has the greater appeal, finiteness or infinity? Which is the higher thought, to believe in limits or illimitability? Which makes more sense and, furthermore, if an individual can perceive or at least think in terms of an infinite existence, does this not preclude a finite one?

Understanding which of these concepts is correct is of paramount importance because it is the concept which serves as a basis for living. To believe in a finite universe will yield finite results and actions. Likewise with a belief in infinity. The former will manifest finite, limiting, restrictive thoughts and conditions. The latter will result in a life style which is unlimited, expansive and expanding, totally unrestricted. The former, therefore, will yield bondage. The latter, freedom. To choose finiteness will result in stagnation. To choose infinity will result in continued growth and development and ascension to higher plateaus of existence and levels of learning.

At this point it is probably unquestionably vivid that this book centers itself in the concept of infinity for, from the author's standpoint, it appears to be the only valid concept of existence. Personal experience will show that man's potentials are unlimited because any individual has only to assert himself to realize that he is capable of reaching any frontier to which his thought can carry him. There are no limits, just those created by a limit-conscious mind.

The preceding statement has been proven by countless numbers of individuals throughout history. A simple personal observation will show that generic man, as expressed in male and female forms, has overcome and conquered seemingly impossible tasks. When one person utters the statement that something cannot be done, as certainly as the sun shines, another individual will challenge and conquer that which allegedly couldn't be done and, therefore, totally decimate such thoughts of impossibility and limitation.

No challenge has forever continued unconquered. Man will never reach the limits of his abilities because there are no limits. He has proven that. He lives in an infinite universe, and he is infinite in potential. He is inherently free and has only to assert himself to realize his freedom – one aspect of his divinity.

As man has proven his ability to conquer challenges, he needs to continue in the same manner. There are still obstacles which, until overcome, inhibit him from experiencing more beautiful life styles. One such obstacle is the concept of finiteness.

BIRTH – DEATH

Man of today survives within a dungeon. In such a state of captivity he cannot fly. Perhaps the greatest tragedy of all,

Richard Andrew King

however, is that he has been enslaved for so long he has little cognizance of his potential for flight. For ages he has grown accustomed to the walls of his cell, so much so that he perceives them as an integral part of his life. His environment is one of dungeons and chains, although he may refer to them as castles and ribbons. It is unfortunate he does not know that beyond the walls of material existence there exists a way of life whose majesty far exceeds his mortal understanding.

These walls of his captivity are nothing more than his concepts of birth, death, time and space. They are the shackles of his imprisonment, and he will never know true freedom until he breaks them.

The current thought of existence is that an individual is born, lives a life of a certain number of years and then dies, returning to dust. His birth date and death date are the boundaries of his life – the entrance and exit to his life's drama. But these two dates, as auspicious as they seem to be, are nothing more than the garments of finite thought. They are the manifestation of man's imprisonment, the epitome of limitation. Yet, they are conceived to be a natural part of living, a verity of existence. Perhaps so, but such a belief is commensurate with finiteness, not infinity; with mortality, not immortality.

Infinity means that which is endless, limitless, boundless. If an individual functionally lived in a consciousness of infinity he could not die because infinity, by definition, has no boundaries, no stopping points. Man, therefore, would have no end, i.e., he would not die, because death, by definition, is an end and, furthermore, it is the antithesis of life. By rejecting death and all concepts of finite thought, man acquires the countenance of infinity, and this countenance manifests itself in a condition of immortality, i.e., that which is not mortal, exempt from death.

Generally speaking, man has not been able to resolve this event called death. He doesn't know that the reason it exists is that he currently dwells in the region of finite thought and death is a result of such thought. Trying desperately to explain it, he has labeled it as a part of life and left it at that.

However, death is no more a part of life than darkness is a part of light. It is a manifestation of mortal, finite thought. Nothing more. Man undergoes the experience called death because he has not functionally lived in the consciousness of life and infinity – levels of consciousness where the most minute thought of death is totally non-existent.

Life is life – a state of vital, moving, dynamic energy. It is an expression of divine intelligence. It is creation. It is God consciously realized. It is.

Death, on the other hand, is an absence of energy and vitality. It is destruction, the end result of decay. It is the non-realization of God.

Richard Andrew King

Life and death cannot mix. The former is reality; the latter is the absence of reality. To explain death as a part of life is nothing more than unadulterated deception. Man has been deceived too long. It is time he destroyed the veils enshrouding his understanding and awakened to the reality of his existence in immortality. He must be courageous enough to stand in the arena amid turbulent shouts from the death-oriented mass consciousness and proclaim fervently his dominion in life. Perhaps he will stand alone, but at least he will stand free.

Death has also been explained as a door to life. This analogy recognizes that life is eternal but it fails in its understanding of life. Death is no door to eternal life any more than an academic letter grade of "F," symbolizing failure, is a mark of excellence.

Death must be understood for what it represents – an inadequacy to fully live in the consciousness of life. It is anathema to man's well-being. It is no entrance to eternality. The only door to life is life.

The analogy has been used before that death is merely an obstacle to overcome. It is a hurdle which must be jumped, a mountain that must be climbed, a mark that must be surpassed. Obstacle. Obstacle. Obstacle. This is the nature of the event called death.

Because the expression of Divine Perfection necessitates a functional understanding of life and only life, the student, if he is to reach a state of such enlightenment, must develop his consciousness to a level commensurate with such illumination, just as he would have to do in learning other things.

For example, assume an individual suffers from headaches caused by tension. If he learns to relax, he avoids tension and the headache never occurs. In this instance the obstacle to be overcome was tension; the headache being its manifestation. When the individual consciousness was elevated from the "tension level" to the "relaxation level," the experience drastically changed from one of discomfort to one of comfort.

But with this transition should also come the understanding that tension need not be a part of life. In fact, as the "relaxation consciousness" maintains itself, tension will remain non-existent in the individual's experience. Yet, until it is overcome, it remains a reality of existence. However, when perceived correctly it is nothing except the result of a lack of harmony and peace.

The same is true of death. It, ostensibly, is a fact of existence. However, when the "life consciousness" increases to a level above the "death consciousness," death will be seen for what it really is – a manifestation of limited, lifeless thought. It is not really a part of life as expressed in eternal form. Once individual consciousness is centered in the concept of life, death, as a personal experience, will be relegated to the domain of long, past-distant memory.

The key word then regarding death is "obstacle." The student should consider it only in this manner and definitely seek to

Richard Andrew King

54

overcome it. As he accepts the challenge, persists in the struggle and records a victory, he will reflect a functional understanding of life. Thus, by his demonstrative ability he will have proven himself worthy to receive the title possessed by all who have met and conquered the same challenge. That title, "Master."

If death is nothing more than an obstacle to overcome, then what of birth? Surely, if man does not die, he cannot be born, for birth is the bringing forth of life, and if man already lives, his existence obviates birth. It might be said that birth is the means whereby an individual who has lost consciousness of life regains it. Birth is the resurgence of the rejuvenated spirit.

> Death is only as a cloud covering mortal eyes;
> Death lies.
> The truth is not as we would see,
> for death is but a lie; life, Reality.
>
> Death is only as a cloud,
> a passing shadow, a mixture of winds,
> a shroud before Truth until dissolved by Truth.
>
> A cloud is only a veil passing before the sun.
> Death is only a thought
> passing through the corridors of mind.

The Karate Consciousness

Clouds only lie.

Men can fly above clouds

where they are nonexistent,

where there is only Light

shining upon a crystalline sea of Reality.

The act of birth is the opening of the door to the consciousness of life. Death is the closing of that door. One belief of today advocates that this opening (birth) and the closing (death) continue in perpetuity until the individual can elevate his consciousness to a level in which birth and death are nonexistent. Until such time that the individual can reach such a state of enlightenment, however, he will continue to lead an indefinite number of lives. He will die, be reborn, etc.

This concept of reincarnation does have merit. How, for instance, can it be accounted for that one person may have a natural knack for speaking many different languages; another an affinity for a certain geographical location; another an intense desire to excavate ancient ruins in order to study the past, and still another the uncanny ability to describe, in detail, the rooms of a house in which he'd never been, which is decades old and even in another country? Are all of these instances the result of memory of other times, places, people or previously learned activities? Perhaps.

Richard Andrew King

To further the argument, however, is it conceivable that such a grand creation of the life force, as man is, could only have one, single, solitary existence? What does the inner voice say?

If the principle of reincarnation is valid, and all Saints say it is so, i.e., that reincarnation is a fact of life, each of us would then be an "entity in transition," a living being continually involved in change and/or movement. Within this transition cycle, which Saints refer to as the "Wheel of Transmigration," we could be progressing, regressing, or stagnating at any one time, and the process could be, not just for fifty, seventy-five, one-hundred or five-hundred years but forever, at least until we ascend to those higher levels of reality which transcend time and space.

THE CONTINUUM

Given this understanding of reincarnation, the student would be well served to consider viewing all life, i.e., the life process, as a continuum or a channel of endless experience and himself as an "entity in transition" through it.

This has important meaning for him because it expands his consciousness from finiteness to infinity. It also has personal developmental ramifications, for what an individual does or does not do today as far as his growth is concerned will affect what and where he is one, two, five, seven hundred years from now, ad infinitum.

The Karate Consciousness

For instance, if he is impatient in this life phase and he takes no action to grow out of it, he will be just as impatient in his next life or life phase. He will continue to possess this attribute until he overcomes it – life phase after life phase. Too, as long as the student maintains a consciousness of death, he will neither break nor overcome the aforementioned birth-death cycle and advance himself to that realm where only a consciousness of life exists.

> Surmount the obstacle death and pass to sky –
> to that boundless realm of life
> where man can fly, soar,
> and extend his mind to Son;
> where he will know the glory
> of a limitless distance run;
> where he will feel the majesty
> of a soul in ethereal flight,
> and bathe in the luminescence
> and the shattering brilliance of the Light;
> where he will perceive forever
> in the Mind of this boundless sea,
> that he is divine creation –
> Beautiful, Perfect, Alive and Free!

Richard Andrew King

PLANNING

There is a saying, "Plan your work and work your plan." This is a good piece of advice for just about any goal-oriented task. Efficiency comes with organization; organization is the direct result of planning. Such preparation is a definite key to success.

For example, if a person were about to embark on a journey to a specific destination he would, in order to make the trip as efficacious as possible, have delineated his route either in his mind or on paper. He may possess a road map if traveling by land or, if it is an inter-galactic journey, a computer readout of various star systems. Whatever the means he will have some type of plan, and success will come as the plan is followed.

With his expanding consciousness of infinity, the student will do well to incorporate the planning concept into his life style if he has not already done so. Knowing that even when he undergoes the transition of death he will be reborn until he can overcome it, he begins to perceive his life as a never-ending series of events and experiences. He, therefore, will desire to plan his journey through infinity just as he would plan a trip across town or across the country. That is, he will plan if he has some idea of individual growth and understanding.

GROWTH PATTERNS

When we speak of planning our journey through infinity, we are referring to planning our spiritual growth as we continue in the consciousness of life. How high in our thought and demonstrative ability can we go? This is obviously an unanswerable question, for if it could be answered, there would be a limit to our growth, but infinity, of course, has no limits.

We grow by learning. Therefore, when we study karate we should do so knowing that the end result is growth – personal, spiritual edification. Oftentimes, karate is studied only for fighting skills; self-development is discarded. This is indicative of the horizontal growth process.

HORIZONTAL GROWTH PATTERN

An individual who studies karate simply for its animal weaponry would be identified with a horizontal growth pattern. This type of structure is one whose learning is of extrinsic design, i.e., outside the individual developmental center. Very little of the knowledge acquired when utilizing this pattern assists the student in elevating his consciousness. It may expand it laterally but not vertically.

What is horizontal or lateral expansion? It is an amplification of individual consciousness relative only to a specific level or subject of worldly existence. The focus is not on growth but on learning everything possible, or as much as possible, about the immediate life-phase plateau. Hence, growth is stunted.

For example, the student who concentrates strictly on learning combative skills may well expand his consciousness of fighting but such an expansion does not assist in his spiritual growth, generally speaking. There are levels of consciousness in which combative concepts do not exist, and in order to reach such plateaus the student would have to abandon his continued concentration on combative prowess and transfer his attention to his spiritual development. Otherwise, he would slow down or even halt his growth. The following diagram helps to illustrate this point.

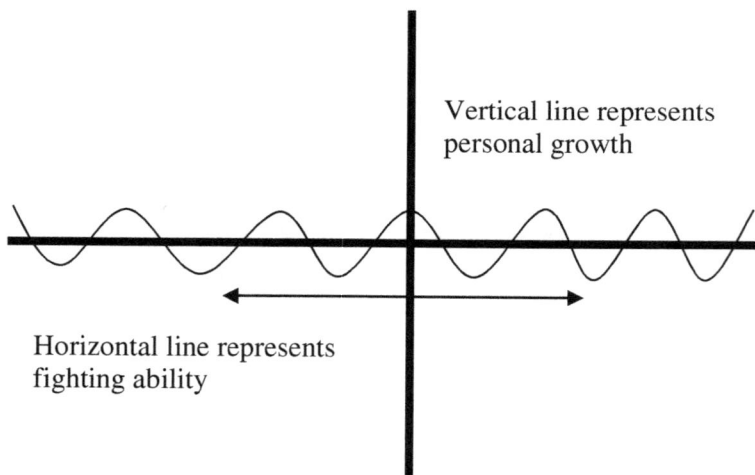

Vertical line represents personal growth

Horizontal line represents fighting ability

The horizontal line in the diagram above is indicative of the student's combative progress. By concentrating on fighting in this manner, he increases his consciousness horizontally or laterally but does not increase it on the vertical plane, which is the one responsible for an increase in the ascending quality of his life.

VERTICAL GROWTH PATTERN

Obviously, then, the vertical growth pattern is the one upon which the student should be focused. The wavy line in the diagram below is concerned with this structure.

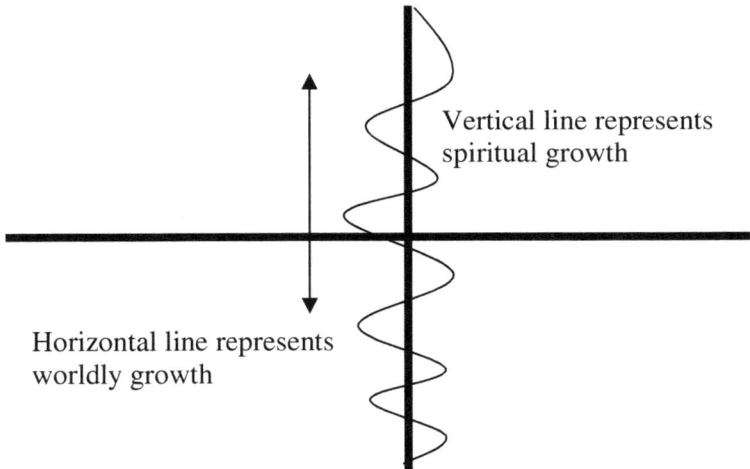

Vertical line represents spiritual growth

Horizontal line represents worldly growth

Vertical expansion is an amplification of individual consciousness relative to personal growth. By concentrating on his vertical growth, the student avoids focusing his learning energies on one level or subject because he realizes it is inhibitive and deleterious to his ascent. Rather, he draws only enough from each level or subject to raise himself above it. In other words, he is totally centered in the concept of continually elevating his consciousness.

Richard Andrew King

Because he has not only planned his life-phase (in general terms) but his existence (as far as his understanding will carry him), he is cautious of learning those things which do not further his purpose or which would cause him either to stagnate or be diverted from the vertical path, i.e., those things detaining him from advancing to higher plateaus of life.

While a horizontal growth pattern may be referred to as extrinsic, the vertical is intrinsic. It is focused on individual growth, and the best way to insure such growth is to go *within*, to traverse the inward path to divine self-realization. It is this inward journey and the discoveries made upon the way which will increase the individual's vibration rate and effectuate an increase in consciousness.

VIBRATION

At this point it might be helpful to discuss this theory of vibration as it relates to the subject at hand. All life is in movement. This rate of movement creates a vibration. The more rapid the movement, the higher the vibration. A common rock, for instance, appears to be stagnate. Yet, it is moving in a vibratory sense.

Man, when viewed as a conscious entity, might also be considered as having a vibration rate yielding a certain frequency designation. As his vibration rate increases so, concomitantly, does his frequency. This is applicable to his body as well as his thought. In fact, his body will vibrate at a frequency no higher than his thought. The higher, more spiritual his thought, the higher his vibration rate and frequency.

In relation to our growth patterns, the horizontal one has a constant vibration rate. Because such a rate is derived from the level of thought, it follows that the mental capacity and illumination remain static. Hence, no growth, no increase in consciousness, no enhancement in the quality of life.

The vertical pattern, on the other hand, is totally non-static. The vibration rate is constantly moving and, relating to individual consciousness, hopefully in an upward direction. Therefore, the individual has the opportunity to increase his consciousness of life and experience greater manifestations of the life force. He can, in other words, grow.

This is another reason why learning only the combative techniques of karate is not in the best interests of the student. It is inhibitive to personal growth. And in order to realize his divine perfection, every person must be afforded the most beneficial avenue for growth and development.

The world consciousness today is overly centered in the horizontal pattern. As emphasis is changed to the vertical, and individuals begin to actively demonstrate their concern for self growth and development, the global consciousness will be elevated – not through luck or good fortune but through increased vibration.

Richard Andrew King

These horizontal and vertical growth patterns are given for the purpose of illustration. It should not be assumed that they are the only growth patterns. Too, it should be noted that our lives are never centered completely in one or the other but are a mixture of the two. The emphasis, however, for those sentient beings who desire to express life to greater degrees should, unequivocally, be centered within the concept of the vertical.

To always strive for and think the higher thought; to continually seek the more enlightened consciousness; to increase personal vibration – this is the more meaningful understanding of the serious karateka and student of life.

PLATEAUS

In discussing personal growth there is another concept which deserves attention and this is the idea of the "plateau." The expansion of individual consciousness doesn't proceed at a uniform rate of speed. It takes time for a person to ingest, absorb and assimilate the knowledge and other data needed for the growth process within the life system. In other words, a person ascending in consciousness will not generally follow the pattern in diagram "A" below but rather he would follow that in diagram "B."

Diagram A

Straight Line Vertical Growth; No Stops.

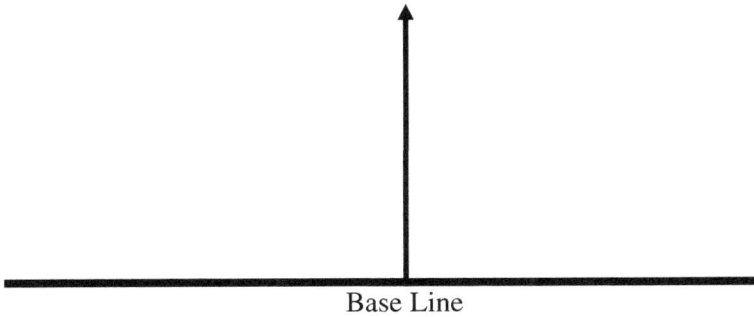

Base Line

Diagram B

Vertical Growth Pattern with Plateaus

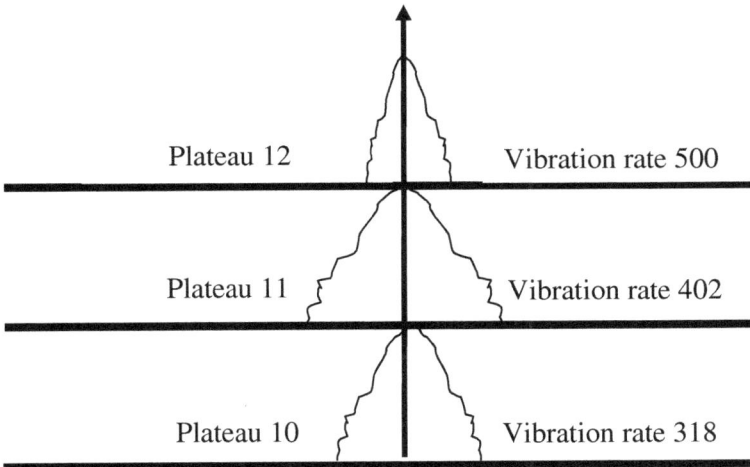

Plateau 12   Vibration rate 500

Plateau 11   Vibration rate 402

Plateau 10   Vibration rate 318

The preceding diagram is illustrative of the plateau concept. The plateau and vibration rate numbers are arbitrary. The growth pattern can be traced in the following manner:

Richard Andrew King

Arriving at plateau #10, the student acquired a vibration rate of 318 where his energies leveled off as represented by the base line intersected by the wavy lines. It took time to assimilate all he had learned at this level before acquiring a consciousness high enough to enable him to reach plateau #11 (vibration rate 402). Here he remained longer than on #10 before acquiring the ability and enlightenment to advance to plateau #12 (vibration rate 500) where he spent little time prior to advancing upward, ad infinitum.

His growth, as can be seen in this diagram, is one of learning, rising, leveling off; learning, rising, leveling off, etc. The term to signify this procedure is called *plateauing*. It is a common pattern of growth development.

What are these plateaus? They are levels of existence, states of consciousness, rates of spiritual vibration, life phases. Each plateau has characteristics all its own. However, the higher the vibration rate and plateau number, the greater the life experience.

For example, plateau #11 would be more spiritual than #10; #12 more than #11 and so forth. The greater the height, the greater the expression of the life force.

These plateaus may be divided into major and minor levels, the latter being the parts which comprise the whole. For example, assume you are walking up an eleven story building. Each story is a major level. However, in order to make the transition from one level (story) to the next you must walk up the stairs. These stairs

The Karate Consciousness

represent minor levels. Each step is higher than the one preceding it but just one step is not enough to get you to the next floor or major level. It takes climbing a number of steps or ascensions to minor levels to bridge the gap between major ones.

In reference to our growth the idea is the same. It requires the "climbing of a set of stairs" or the continual ascension to minor levels to reach major plateaus. Each step is, of course, an increased state of consciousness manifesting concomitant degrees of functional demonstrability.

Another way of describing major and minor plateaus would be to use the analogy of the educational system. The first level is generally preschool, followed by kindergarten, elementary, junior high, high school, college, graduate and post graduate levels. All of these represent major plateaus. Yet, within each "school" there are grades which comprise the entire level. Elementary school, for example, when viewed as a major level, has six minor levels – grades one through six. Similar gradations may also be accounted for in higher levels of the educational process.

Life can also be viewed in this manner. However, the levels are not quite as distinct. In application of this concept of plateaus we may think of our earth experience as a major level, understanding, of course, that there are lower and higher plateaus of existence where the educational curriculum is drastically different.

Richard Andrew King

For instance, our earth experience, regardless of how many life times or life phases it incorporates, may be considered as a school of mortal, i.e., human thought. The goal of the student would be to work his way from the lower more animalistic levels of mortal thought to the higher levels until he could graduate from this major level, the plateau of mortality, and enter the level of immortality. What lies beyond the plateau of immortality can only be speculative at this point. However, in contemplation of the learning at hand, the graduation exercise from mortality to immortality is referred to as *ascension*.

This *ascension* is obviously not the result of a moment's work. It is the culminating experience of many moments of smaller ascensions. Just as an individual encased in mortal consciousness cannot ascend from ground level to the top of our eleven story building (discussed earlier) in one leap, but must make a number of smaller ascensions via the climbing of separate stairs, so the ascent from mortality to immortality involves climbing one step at a time, i.e., elevating the consciousness one thought at a time. It is a process demanding patience and persistence.

DEATH – NO ENTRANCE

It was noted earlier that death is not a door to life. By the same token, it is not an entrance to a higher or lower plateau. Simply by going to sleep at night an individual doesn't arise a better person, a refreshed and revitalized one, maybe, but not one necessarily more wise or loving than the day before. In order to acquire the characteristics of love and wisdom he must work at them daily, and his progress along these lines and every other line will be made and measured during each conscious moment, not each morning after a night's rest.

Death, in a traditional explanation, may be likened to falling asleep. Birth, the coming out of death into life, may be likened to waking up. However, neither possesses any magic. The individual must still meet the same challenges he had prior to "going asleep" until he can overcome them. He could die a thousand times but until he gets seriously down to the business of elevating his consciousness, he will make no progress in terms of his spiritual growth.

The main thing to remember in all of this discussion is that this earth experience, i.e., mortality, is to be challenged just as any other subject or task is challenged. And it must be overcome. The goal is to graduate and ascend to the next major energy level, the next one after that, etc., until the plateau of immortality is attained where individual form will be that of pure light.

COMMENCEMENT REQUISITES

Ascending to any level, be it major or minor, requires an increase in vibration, which is the subsequent result of an increase in consciousness. In other words, as our consciousness level increases, we experience more harmonious and beautiful expressions of the life force.

In order to elevate his consciousness the student will be greatly benefited if he thinks of his Being in terms of energy and light. The more he increases his energy, the more light he emanates. And, as he becomes an "enlightened" individual, he will perceive greater dimensions of the universe. Each plateau to which he advances will possess a higher energy level and degree of luminosity. He cannot reach these levels unless his own Being is vibrating at a rate commensurate with the level to which he is advancing.

For example, an individual cannot teach at the university level unless he has the appropriate degrees or credentials; an aspiring athlete cannot join the ranks of the professionals unless he possesses and demonstrates ability which is coincidental with the caliber of a professional. Likewise, a student of life cannot dwell on a plateau of higher life experience until he has elevated his consciousness to that plateau.

The entire process, therefore, is one of continual consciousness elevation. This will be recognized as spiritual growth, and as the student ascends to progressively higher levels, he will acquire and manifest light, the natural result of an increase in energy and vibration.

The Karate Consciousness

MOMENTUM

Consciousness expansion, however, is not an easy task. If it were, the mass consciousness would be higher than it is. In addition to many of the concepts and principles he must learn in order to advance vertically, the student will do well to consider this concept of momentum.

Momentum is a marked degree of energy in motion. It can be salutary to individual progress but also deleterious, given different circumstances.

For instance, in a football game, as in other athletic contests, the team with the greatest degree of momentum is usually in the driver's seat. Oftentimes, such a condition seems invincible – a desirable position for the team with the ball.

However, on the other side of the coin, too much momentum may be detrimental. A gymnast may not be able to perform a particular movement perfectly if he or she generates more momentum than the exercise or movement calls for.

It is the same in the accomplishment of all tasks or problems. Perfect execution requires perfect momentum – the right amount of energy coincidental with the needs of the exercise. It can neither be excessive nor diminutive. It must be perfect.

Richard Andrew King

However, it does "need to be," i.e., it needs to exist. An individual cannot grow if he has no momentum because growth is movement, movement requires energy, and vertical elevation especially requires a continual increase in energy. No movement, no growth. It's that simple.

This movement is not necessarily physical. It is mental; it is spiritual. It is active thought moving upwards. It is consciousness progressing from intellectuality to functionability and demonstrability. It is energy in transition from materiality to light. It is individual ascension from mortality – the consciousness of death, to immortality – the consciousness of life.

STOP AND GO VERSUS FLOW

Momentum is most efficacious to individual growth if it is in a state of perpetual flow. It loses its effectiveness if it is stopped, in which case it must be regenerated. This latter condition not only requires time but increased thrusts of energy. It is much easier to keep the flow going than it is to stop it and, consequently, have to rebuild it. Therefore, regarding momentum, the student should consider it as a flowing process, not a "stop and go" one.

The concept of momentum assumes considerable dimensions when associated with the idea of life as a continuum. As discussed earlier, an individual may experience many life phases until he can consciously elevate himself to the status of immortality. Until he reaches this goal, he cannot be indolent or remiss in its application.

For example, he must never cease trying to extricate himself from the mortal consciousness of life because his efforts may well advance him to the next major level of learning at any time. If he cannot elevate his consciousness high enough to reach the next level this time around, by maintaining his momentum, even through death, he will be that much farther along when he awakens to life again.

From age one to age sixty-seven, ninety, one hundred thirty or five hundred, growth is a perpetual activity. In contrast to an individual's "working years" there is no retirement for a student of life because to retire is to cease activity when, contrastingly, spiritual elevation demands it. Thus, the student is admonished to consider strongly this concept of momentum – not in terms of "stop and go" but perpetual flow.

MOMENTUM MAINTENANCE

The question then arises, "How is this flow maintained?" Perhaps one of the most salient answers is for each student to be centered in the process of being "Better today than he was yesterday and making plans for becoming better tomorrow than he is today." "Better" is equated to having a higher level of consciousness, of generating a higher rate of vibration.

Richard Andrew King

In comparing today's consciousness with yesterday's we can see where we have been. By comparing today with what we would like tomorrow we can see where we should go or what we should do to transform our desire into actuality. By making plans for tomorrow we tie future time into the present. Therefore, everything remains in continuity. If we did not plan our goals for tomorrow, we would awake in the morning not knowing where we are going or what we must do. The flow would have been broken; our momentum halted until we could rebuild it.

We must also be aware that in stopping the flow we may not want to start it again because of the effort involved. It is, therefore, much easier and more beneficial for us to continue maintaining the momentum flow. As long as it is operative, it will carry us along to our destination. But once terminated it will be non-effectual. Therefore, for our well-being we must live in the fullness of continually increasing our consciousness so that we may maintain our momentum and arrive at our ultimate destination – the level of immortality – as efficiently and quickly as possible.

KARATE: SYSTEM OF SELF-DEVELOPMENT

As life is a continuum and this earth an institution of learning within it, so karate is one course offered in the curriculum of this particular institution. It is one part of the whole, and it would be incorrect to conceive of it in any other way.

The Karate Consciousness

The proper perspective of karate is that of a system of self-development, one avenue enabling the student to expand his consciousness. To perceive it as merely a system of animal warfare would be to depreciate its higher value to mankind.

As mentioned before, however, karate has been associated too much with animal and material prowess. Subsequently, the karate consciousness vibrates at a level of such thought. This is not good for individual growth and development, and because of such a condition, students of the art are missing out on a plethora of abundance in the form of knowledge, learning and growth which could be theirs if the karate consciousness were centered in spiritual edification.

To study the art only to acquire fighting skills is to go to the well for a bucket of water and return with only a spoonful. It is an inefficient use of time and energy. However, to travel to the well for a bucket full of water and return with a full container is efficiency. It is also wisdom and prudence because a bucketful of water will sustain life longer than a mere spoonful.

To perceive karate as a system of self-development rather than a system of animal weaponry is to return with a bucket full of water from the well. As the student seeks more of life, he receives more, but he must first seek. Life is truly wonderful but, like the water, in order to receive its blessing, it must first be sought. Karate offers one avenue for the seeker of water, and in seeking it he will

Richard Andrew King

be benefited if he holds dear to his heart these famous words of Ulysses: *To strive, to seek, to find, but not to yield!*

SUMMARY

Life is infinite. It is a continuum. Birth and death have no significance except in the concept of finiteness. They are the manifestation of a mind encased in mortality, the consciousness of death. Man's goal at this level of existence is to rise above death, to breech the walls of mortality and enter into immortality – a consciousness of eternal, infinite life.

In effectuating this transition the karateka must study the art with his attention directed to personal growth and spiritual edification. He must study to increase his consciousness vertically, not horizontally, and thereby elevate his vibration until he radiates a mantle of light – the clothing of his divinity.

In this growth process he must learn certain lessons. One is, obviously, to assume a mental posture of life and only life. Yet, there are others.

Chapter 4

THOUGHT

Of all the lessons he must learn;

Of all the wisdom he is taught;

Man must come to realize his life

Is but the manifestation of his thought;

That thought can wield the power

And the force to set him free,

And elevate his consciousness to fact

That he is master of his destiny.

Richard Andrew King

Thought is, arguably, the most dynamic force in the universe. It is the essence of individual Being and the substance of consciousness. It is the medium through which man traverses that territory from mortality to immortality. Its manifestations can be a blessing or a hindrance; its resultant vibrations a joy or discordant experience.

The importance, power and manifestations of thought cannot be underestimated by the karateka and student of life. To do so would be a most treacherous and myopic deficiency. To avoid indulgence in constructive, positive, dynamic and edifying thought is a deleterious act in relation to personal growth. In judgement of such action the individual is penalized through the self-construction of his own prison walls. Through his negligence of divine thought he fabricates the shackles which bind him to the ground and, thereby, preclude his flight into the dazzling clear skies of freedom.

Elevation of individual consciousness is a direct result of the elevation of individual thought. Therefore, as the student is desirous of expanding and elevating his consciousness and expediting his ascent to higher plateaus of existence, he must become "thought-conscious." He must learn to live in the realm of Thought.

THOUGHT VERSUS BODY CONSCIOUSNESS

The karate consciousness of today, however, is centered, not in "thought consciousness" but in "body consciousness." Animal prowess, fighting skills, self-defense techniques, exercises, etc., all of which are expressions of physical form, receive the majority of attention as far as the art is concerned. This is because karate has been made an end in itself rather than the means to an end. Personal glorification has received too much attention; personal edification too little when, in actuality, the latter should be that which receives the greatest consideration and concentration.

Part of the purpose of karate is to stimulate the thinking process, show the relationship of thought to action and illustrate, through demonstrability, how an increase or correct utilization of the thought process brings and/or yields a greater degree of personal control, poise, power, strength, flexibility, stamina, harmony, peace, etc. The learning required to generate these characteristics or the principles behind the learning may then be transferred to daily activities to render an overall increase in the quality of life.

For example, in order to increase the efficiency of a bodily movement, the body must first be relaxed. If tense, it does not have the capability to flow smoothly in perfect rhythm. Yet, relaxation is a mental process, not a physical one. If the mind is relaxed, the body will follow. Thus, when a karateka learns to relax mentally, his bodily control will increase. If percipient, he

Richard Andrew King

will see that relaxation yields efficiency. Then when confronted with any problem in or out of the karate atmosphere, he can transfer what he has learned to the situation at hand in order to effectuate a solution.

On the job, for instance, he may find himself with too much work to do in too short a time. By mentally relaxing he allows the intelligence needed to solve the problem to flow smoothly through him and, thus, his work will be enhanced. If, on the other hand, he tenses up, his intellect cannot function properly and he will probably find himself and the work he has to do in a state of confusion.

"Body consciousness," however, envelopes greater dimensions than simply the expression of physical weaponry and techniques. Contemporary scientific understanding attributes five senses to the body: sight, sound, taste, touch and smell. Although linked to the mind, these sensations are attributable to the body. An individual who centers his attention in them is said to be sensuous (relating to the senses). Such a condition can be deleterious to personal growth because mortal, bodily sensations do not and cannot give a full account of existence. They are limiting and finite.

For example, the human auditory mechanism is capable of receiving all sounds within a specific frequency range. Yet, a dog can perceive sounds beyond the human's capacity. It would, therefore, be a grave mistake for any individual to assume that all

The Karate Consciousness

life is defined and described within the realm of his limited perception.

It is this state of believing that man's senses "tell it all' and, therefore, saturating himself in sense, that gives rise to the phrase "body consciousness." But man must relinquish this propensity because sense, sensation and sensuality are finite. Their indulgence restricts the expansion of individual consciousness because if consciousness knows nothing else or can perceive nothing else it will not seek to know anything else. Therefore, its growth is proscribed.

It is for this reason that man must become more "thought conscious." In doing so he will begin to rise above sense, step out of finiteness and into infinity. The quality of his life will then be increased because his consciousness will perceive more of existence. He will have a greater understanding of his Being and, therefore, move closer to the realization of his Divine Perfection.

In order to expand and elevate his consciousness by elevating his thought, the student should utilize his mental faculties to entertain, intellectually understand, and functionally demonstrate expressions of the life force associated with spirit, love, life, peace, harmony, completeness, atonement, integrity, discipline, strength, gentleness, beauty, purity, intellect, understanding, control, creativity, perfection. It is man's thought focused on these concepts which will elevate his understanding and increase the actual expression of them in his own life, all of which will result in

Richard Andrew King

a higher, more ethereal consciousness. To be all that these concepts indicate is to truly be enlightened. The mastery of them will further qualify the individual to receive even higher teachings, but those catalogued above are of primary importance. They are prerequisites for graduation to the next level.

RECOGNITION AND REALIZATION

Throughout the ages thought has been recognized and realized as the most dynamic force in the universe. It is not a fashion which is in this year and out the next. It is an eternal garment of the life force – always in vogue with an expanding mind. The following list is a brief account of a few individual perceptions of thought throughout the ages. The similitude is quite interesting.

I think, therefore I am.

~ Descartes

As a man thinketh in his heart, so is he.

~ Solomon

A man is what he thinks all day long.

and

Thought rules the world.

~ Ralph Waldo Emerson

Thought is the master of all forms of energy.

and

Every creation of man, whether it be good of bad,

is created first in a thought pattern.

~ Napoleon Hill & E. Harold Keown

Dynamic thinkers rule the world.

and

The human mind is the greatest instrument in the world.

~ Anthony Norvell

The demands of God appeal to thought only.

You embrace your body in your thought.

We must form perfect models in thought and

look at them continually, or we shall never

carve them out in grand and noble lives.

~ Mary Baker Eddy

One is a product of one's thinking.

~ Melvin Powers

The law of life is this: 'all things both good and evil

are constructed from an image held in mind'.

and

There is absolutely no such thing as accomplishment

unless it is preceded by a vision of that accomplishment.

~ U. S. Anderson

Richard Andrew King

The abode of man is mind.

and

Mind and matter are related. They are ends of the
same continuum. Mind flows into form ceaselessly.

~ R. Eugene Nichols

Now, reading does not build the mind; thought alone
builds it . . . We should read less and think more if we
would have our minds grow and our intelligence develop.

~ Annie Besant

Seek the life that is of the mind.

and

What we think, we become.

~ Buddha

Reading, after a certain age, diverts the mind too much
from its creative pursuits. Any man who reads too
much and uses his own brain too little falls into
lazy habits of thinking.

~ Albert Einstein

As one can readily perceive from these quotations, thought is and has been regarded as a dynamic force, indeed. It is responsible for creating all that a man is and all that he shall become. It must be reckoned with. Its relationship to the life process must be understood, for it is only in acquiring a functional, not intellectual,

The Karate Consciousness

understanding that each individual will come to know its power for himself. To intellectually know the capability of thought is not enough. Philosophizing will not get the job done. It requires demonstrability, and such an activity is only acquired through the correct perception and utilization of thought.

CAUSE AND EFFECT

The student will begin to rise higher in his expression of the life force when he comes to realize that nothing is coincidental, that every effect has a cause and, conversely, every cause has an effect. The understanding of this law of cause and effect is absolutely essential for the individual who desires to become a master of life.

To become a master of anything, be it painting, writing, singing, dancing, selling, building, living, etc., the artisan must understand the causes that produce the desired effect. Without this knowledge he can never be consistent, but it is consistency which proves his ability and artistry. To be able to perform a specific task again and again and again is the mark of a master.

Therefore, in relation to his personal growth, if the student desires to elevate his consciousness and expression of the life force, he must work within this law of cause and effect. He must realize that thought is cause and the resultant expression or activity is effect, that nothing that happens to him can be described as either chance or luck; that all effects have a cause.

Richard Andrew King

For example, if he desires to be a more peaceful person, he must know there is only one way for him to be so and that is to create the desired effect by initiating the correct thought. He will not become peaceful by chance but by purposefully, intentionally and deliberately generating peaceful thoughts and actions.

If he wants to become a Black Belt, he must first think and, using his imagination, visualize himself as a Black Belt. If he desires to be a world famous concert pianist, he must think and visualize himself as such. If he wants to be a champion in any sport, thinking and visualizing himself as winning is critical to his achievement. And, most importantly, if he desires to transcend the worldly realm of the warrior and become a mystical master, he must begin by knowing that he has already arrived. He does this through his thought, imagination and visualization.

It is this attitude of "taking charge" of his personal growth that will yield a status of mastery. To "take charge" is not an external process. It is an internal one. To become a master the student must relinquish all propensities of placing the responsibility on some other person, place, thing, situation, condition or environment for his status. He must assume responsibility for his own development and condition, not because this is a nice thing to do but because it is the right thing to do; it is the truth of his existence. He is the creator of what he is. He is responsible for what he has accomplished or not accomplished. He can look to no other source but himself. It all starts with the mind and his thoughts.

The Karate Consciousness

Looking only to himself for his accomplishments and his growth can be, and is, a comforting thought. In doing so the individual becomes self-reliant, a characteristic he must possess to achieve mastery. If, for instance, he is currently not expressing abundance, he knows that he is responsible for such a condition but, likewise, and this is the great understanding, he can change it. He can experience abundance in his life by altering his thought. How? Simply by holding the concept of abundance in his mind until it manifests in his experience as effect or reality. The thought of abundance is cause. The expression of it in his life is effect. This is an immutable law – first cause, then effect. And if the manifestation of abundance does not materialize in this life, it will in a future life. It must according to the divine law of cause and effect. Remember, life is a continuum. Thoughts transcend any one life. They are not limited to this life, to this incarnation only.

As the student grows in his understanding of this principle, he will perceive his entire identity as an expression of cause and effect. If he is irritable and irascible, it is solely because he has maintained or created such concepts in his own mind, for if he fills his entire Being with peace and tranquility, he can never reflect irritability or irascibility. Therefore, if he finds himself in a condition or state of being which is not in keeping with his highest good, he must change his thought process. He must simply clean out his mental cupboard and fill it with new thought substance. Then, as he acts on this thought substance, he will see it take form and become a reality in his experience.

Richard Andrew King

Not only will he see himself in this manner but, likewise, he will perceive the entire race of humanity as the direct manifestation of the thought patterns it creates. The edification of the mass consciousness follows the same principle as the edification of individual consciousness. Change the thought, uplift it, purify it, center it in spirit, love, life, beauty, health, peace, understanding, etc., and the entire spectrum of experience for mankind will change. Why? Because when the mass of humanity goes to its cupboard for sustenance, all that will be there will be the fruits of ethereal consciousness. It is this fruit which supplies the nutrition for its existence.

The karate consciousness is no different. For it to be expressive of greater dimensions of life, the mass thought must be centered in higher concepts of life. Concomitantly, this will be the result of the majority of individual karatekas changing their thoughts, uplifting and edifying them. When this occurs, karate will become more meaningful to society than it currently is.

However, there is a caveat. The student should never wait for the mass consciousness to catch up with his own. He must move forward on his own. If anyone chooses to follow his lead, fine. If not, he must continue the climb by himself. The individual's first obligation is to his own edification, purification, ascent and freedom. It is not incumbent upon anyone to sacrifice himself at the expense of others.

The Karate Consciousness

WORDS AND PICTURES

Understanding that thought is cause, one direct method of individual and mass edification is to make certain that thought is, in itself, elevated. This can be accommodated using words and pictures.

Words are, partially, the structure and substance of the thinking process, just as lumber is the substance of a house. If the words are good, so will be the emanations of the verbal communication process; if the lumber is good, so will be the house, all things being equal. Therefore, to elevate individual consciousness it will be helpful to utilize in thought and speech only words which are congruent with established goals.

For example, words such as hate, envy, jealousy, malice, kill, harm, deceit, can't, limitation, illness, disease, etc., should be afforded little space in an individual's expression. Their utilization only places in motion discordant vibrations. They are, in themselves, a cause. As cause, they produce the same effect. If they are extricated from personal use, they cannot generate a life effect.

By the same token, words signifying higher, more ethereal meaning will generate a similar effect when used genuinely. Examples of these are love, peace, beauty, majesty, grandeur, life, spirit, light, sky, success, can, divinity, loveliness, giving, sharing,

Richard Andrew King

harmony, tranquility, gentleness, soothing, luminous, shining and so forth. The underlying idea is to create a functional vocabulary of nouns, pronouns, verbs, adjectives, adverbs, clauses and phraseology which possesses spiritual or elevated connotations and denotations.

Words, however, do not comprise the entire structure of the thinking process. Mental pictures generated by the imagination also account for much of it. In fact, it may be argued that words only give form to the pictures we see in our minds. Words are a means of conveying and communicating those pictures. Therefore, the visions held in mind must also be edified if consciousness is to be elevated. Visions of giving, loving, sharing, growing, expressing beauty and radiance, accomplishing, creating, etc., should be formed in the mind. As cause, they will create the identical effect in individual experience.

In order to see this law of cause and effect in operation, the student has only to be perceptive and become aware of its effect in his life and environment. It is quite beautiful. and it is also quite exact. No one escapes it and no one can help from being benefited by it if he utilizes it correctly. The student is admonished to understand and apply it in his own life if he is to grow into the fullness of his divinity and become a Master of life.

THOUGHT FIELDS

Pertaining to his growth and well-being, the individual should be acutely aware of, and sensitive to, thought fields – regions of mental forces. Such fields may be extremely beneficial to his growth but, conversely, they may also be quite harmful. To discern one from the other is a most important faculty.

Thoughts create vibrations. The higher the thought the higher the vibration and vice-versa. Generally speaking, the greater the vibration the more beneficial it is to individual Being. However, too much too soon may be harmful.

For example, if a person who had lived in a totally dark cave were suddenly thrown into the light of the noonday sun, the shock would be too much for his system. Even though the light is good and permits him to see more of existence, he must move into the fullness of the light gradually so he can adapt to it – physically, mentally, spiritually.

Low vibrations, those created by thoughts centered in mortal and finite concepts, are dense and heavy to the spirit. They restrict the elevation of individual consciousness and thus bind man to the ground. They are responsible for man's experience of discord and dis-ease – states of being in which he does not nor cannot experience true peace and harmony.

Richard Andrew King

High vibrations, on the other hand, are created by a mind centered in immortal, infinite thought. They are neither dense nor heavy to the spirit and in no way restrict man from elevating his consciousness. They are responsible for rendering man whole, peaceful and harmonious.

Any vibration is not so much intellectually discerned as it is actually felt. When entering a room of people, for example, the sentient and sensitive individual will automatically perceive a vibration. He doesn't have to try to find it. It is there and he will feel it much like he feels running water upon his hand. The vibration may be soothing, uplifting, warm, harmonious, gentle, cold, discordant, inharmonious.

And this is where he must be prudent. If the vibratory force is dense or unwholesome and the person (the one subject to the vibration) is not enlightened or strong enough to overcome or repel it, he should have the common sense to physically extricate himself from the environment because to remain in a discordant thought field is not at all salutary to individual health. There are no moral, ethical or spiritual laws which dictate that a person must submit himself to any situation or environment antithetical to his highest good.

In pursuing that which is best for him, the individual should always establish or occupy environments which are harmonious. Harmony should always be used as the means of measurement.

The Karate Consciousness

In this manner the student need never be concerned about the effect of the thought field upon his Being. Wherever he is in his consciousness, if the environment is harmonious to him, it is right for him. As he grows, he will seek higher thought. Consequently, he will seek those environments which are harmonious at that time and place.

Perhaps the thought fields he dwelled in yesterday are not harmonious to him today, and those of tomorrow may possess more energy than he can currently handle. But as his mind becomes more illumined, he will be able to handle them and so on throughout his journey.

Vibrations are obviously created by other media as well. Music, for instance, can be quite concordant or discordant. The former is soothing and edifying, while the latter can rip asunder the tissues of the mind. In fact, the same is true for all sound waves. The student should be cognizant of them and all vibratory fields, thought or otherwise, if he is to move higher in his consciousness.

MIND

Although his individual mind is important and necessary, man should understand that there is only one Mind, one supreme Intelligence, one Causal Thought Force, one Power within the universe. This intelligence is designated by spelling Mind with a capital "M." It is this Mind which created all individual minds.

Richard Andrew King

Thus, when perceived correctly, all mankind is really one complete whole because it derives its existence, its intellect from this one, primary, causal force.

Too often, however, man is of the belief that he is separate from everyone else. Superficially this is true but exterior appearances are where the differences end. As two trees standing in the forest are separate, both derive their existence, substance and sustenance from the same source. And so it is with man. He is separate only in extrinsic form.

While the mortal aspect of man's character is separation, the immortal is unity. Inherently, all men are one. Furthermore, all life is one complete whole. The causal force that propels an automobile also generates thought, moves the sea, heals the diseased body and sustains the lighted flame of a candle.

It is the nonrealization of this oneness which has perpetuated, among other things, the Power in the Flock Syndrome. By not seeing that he is one with all men, man tries to dominate his fellow man when, if he perceived this principle of unity, he would do all he could to help him, not subordinate him, because in helping one, he helps all; thus, he helps himself. Antithetically, by living in the realm of extrinsic power he undermines the whole and hurts himself. When one suffers, all suffer. When one fails, all fail.

The Karate Consciousness

Man currently dwells too much in the outer; not enough in the inner. Exterior appearance, not interior realization, is the focal point of his concentration.

For example, in the realm of karate there is an over-emphasis on the acquisition and development of fighting skills rather than a balanced emphasis between the manifestations of body, mind and spirit. Consequently, as the student strives to gain only the embellishments of the exterior, he becomes only a shell devoid of substance – an individual lacking substantial identity and integration. If, on the other hand, he learns to become one with the power within, he gains substance, becomes complete and makes definite progress toward the expression of his Divine Perfection.

It is in dwelling in the exterior realm that man creates a feeling of separation, and rightly so, for living in such a manner is to be separate from Mind, the source of all unity, all wholeness, all completeness. It is vital that each student seek this Mind, learn to dwell within its Being and thus allow it to direct his life. By these means he will perceive and express life in grandeur and majesty.

CONTACT

One of the methods of making full contact with this one Mind is to relinquish the habit of concentrating on exterior things, forsake reliance upon appearances, and fortify focus on internal

Richard Andrew King

awareness. Give up the mortal, that which is subject to decay, and seek the immortal, that which explodes with eternal creation.

In order to accomplish this the student must lay aside his human ego, the one which attempts to survive in a world of externalities, and take up his Divine Ego, the one which forever lives in the All of Mind.

The human ego is that which is subject to and expressive of fear, ignorance, pride, arrogance, self-centeredness, lust, greed, hate, jealousy, impatience, animal prowess, poverty, disease, decay and death. Divine Ego is the antithesis of all these. It is expressive of love, intellect, wisdom, understanding, humility, temperance, strength, courage, patience, abundance, completeness, health, vitality and life.

The laying aside of the human ego and the taking up of the Divine is a matter of knowingly surrendering the former and continually and actively centering thought in the latter. "As a man thinketh in his heart, so is he." Thus, by living only in the characteristics of the Divine Ego the student expresses only them. He becomes all that divinity is and he will only know its beauty and loveliness when he reaches this state of Being.

Two other methods of making contact with Mind are prayer and meditation. Traditionally, the former is a process of asking, inquiring, thanking and blessing, while the latter is the focusing of thought on an idea, concept, vision or exercise. Both are extremely beneficial in the pursuit of enlightenment. Man needs to ask this Power within him to come forth, but he also needs to dwell upon the manifestations and expressions it does send forth if he is to render his growth as efficacious as possible. To ask for something and not be appreciative of it when it is given is just as meaningless as trying to create peace within individual consciousness by neglecting to concentrate upon it.

Silence is the great medium for prayer and meditation. Hampered by noises and discordant sounds without, man may have difficulty in concentrating on the communication that occurs within his Being during these periods. Therefore, he must seek silence in order that he truly "hears" and makes no mistakes in the messages he receives.

In establishing this silence the student should separate himself from as much exterior sound and activity as possible. This poses a challenge in today's society because of television, radio, stereo, cell phones, the endless streaming of endless words and music on multiple electronic devices etc., and while these have their place they are contrary to the silence, and their transmissions should be managed more carefully and wisely. Time, meaningful time, should be given every day to the silence, to prayer or meditation.

The physical presence of contemporary devices is not the only barrier to establishing silence. There also exists a psychological one. Man is often too dependent on them. Rather than thinking or meditating, he may watch television, listen to the radio or become

Richard Andrew King

too involved with his cell phone, tablet, computer, etc. Such activities can too often become an habitual pastime, and this is precisely what it is – a passing of time rather than the productive utilization of it. Such a condition is an expression of externality, of appearances, and man will never know the magnificent beauty of the Silence and all of the gifts it brings, especially when combined with prayer and meditation, until he learns to place his external devices and gadgets in their proper place, i.e., on hold, and give thought, prayer and meditation their proper and deserved time.

And what beauty there is in the Silence! There is peace, tranquility, joy, the flow of thought from Mind to the great "I AM," the opportunity to revitalize and energize the spirit, and the environment to travel further into the depths of the Soul. There is true power in silence, and it is the passageway to the one, great, primary, causal force – God.

SUMMARY

As Emerson would say, "Thought rules the world." Yet, in actuality, it rules the universe – the entirety of all that is. This thought is intelligence which flows from and is created by one causal intelligence, Mind. Man is an expression of this Mind and as he relinquishes his mortal human ego and centers his attention on this Divine Ego – the union of his identity with Mind – he will express life in beauty, majesty and grandeur.

The karateka is admonished to think more and functionally learn the relationship of cause to effect, of thought to manifestation. He must continually seek to uplift and edify his thought in order to increase his vibration and expedite his ascent to higher levels of learning and expressions of the life force. He must come to learn through the active demonstration of thought that he is not only free but that he is, unequivocally, the sole undisputed master of his destiny.

The Karate Consciousness

Chapter 5

LOVE

As man extends his wandering palm across a universe of space,
and catapults his mind into the distant realms of infinity;
As he seeks the plains of the great unknown, and strives to soar
within the corridors of the free;
As he struggles up the stairway of his consciousness,
forever gaining sight of mastery, repelling thoughts of
imperfection, denying captive limitation;
As he fights to win, to be heralded as the conqueror of his life,
then, surely, must he come to know that Love is the
manifestation and the Light of the Living Soul.

Richard Andrew King

As thought is the most powerful force in the universe, Love is the greatest of all vibrations. It is the pinnacle of Divine Essence, the elixir of life, the nucleus of infinite wisdom. Love is beauty, and its manifestations are the most exquisite forms of all energy. It is the finest radiance of the Light, and its force is so subtle and yet so powerful it will bring the strongest of men to his knees and elevate the most diminutive of intellects to the highest fields of splendor. Love is the substance of every enlightened consciousness and the fiber of all true greatness.

Love is. It has always been and shall always be. Its supply is infinite; its expression boundless. Its frequency is such that it brings peace to the most discordant vibration and heals the most turbulent disease. Love is the manifestation of the unified soul and the epitome of Divine Perfection.

Love is science. It is not philosophy, although it generally is placed in such a category. When the student understands this he will begin to take great strides in his growth, for he will see that Love is law, and as it is expressed in his individual life his entire existence will assume new meaning and his consciousness will expand to greater dimensions. As surely as one plus one are two, the manifestation of Love in individual Being will increase the vibration of the entity. Higher vibration will yield a commensurate functional understanding of life and such understanding will be translated in terms of beauty, radiance, grandeur and majesty.

The Karate Consciousness

The goal of every student should be to realize this Divine Perfection. To accomplish this he must become a master of life and, concomitantly, to reach such a status he must master the love vibration. There is no equivocating here. Love is the essence of every Master. It is the supernal quality of all living things. Love, therefore, has first priority on the list of prerequisites for graduation to the next major level.

Two of the greatest Masters of recorded history, Buddha and Jesus, have this to say concerning love:

The first meditation is the meditation of love in which you must so adjust your heart that you long for the weal and welfare of all beings, including the happiness of your enemies. ~ Buddha

And thou shalt love the Love thy God with all thy heart, and with all thy soul, and with all thy mind, and with all thy strength; this is the first commandment. And the second is like, namely this, Thou shalt love thy neighbor as thyself. There is none other commandment greater than these. ~ Jesus (KJV-St. Mark 12: 30-31)

It should be noted that in the preceding passages Love is the substance of the first priority, not knowledge, not prestige, not wealth, not celebrity, not high position in society, not ultimate

Richard Andrew King

success in business, but love – first and foremost, now and forever!

As a student and potential master of life, the karateka will do well to consider the teachings of those who have gone before and thus illumined the way. In keeping with these teachings, he must seek to understand and functionally demonstrate Love. This is the highest priority of his study. Moment to moment in thought, word and deed his focus should be on Love.

Such a state of affairs will not only be difficult but it will place the student, especially the conditioned one, in a rather precarious position because, generally speaking, he has been saturated with concepts and goals of, and oriented to, the promotion of Power in the Flock. Love, however, is directly antithetical to such external power because it does not exist to dominate but uplift. Love is totally and completely interested in the welfare of others, not in their subjugation.

Love is power generated internally and expressed outwardly. It is an emanation of the life-giving soul. Love radiates, whereas flock-power absorbs and attempts to gain strength by dominance – a futile activity.

Because Love is such a paramount vibration, its mastery will require considerable effort in most cases. It is not an easy task but it is an essential one. Mortality may exclude it but immortality demands it. The sentient student is, therefore, admonished to practice, practice, practice the fundamentals and concepts of Love to increase and refine his understanding until he elevates his consciousness and demonstrability to mastery.

THE FUNDAMENTALS

Because Love is infinite, it is indescribable in finite terms. One word will not tell all that Love is. Nor will two, three or four. Yet, it is always a good exercise to try because in the attempt we will expand our understanding of it and thus assist in the elevation of our consciousness. Following is such an attempt to catalogue some of the more meaningful aspects of Love.

Edification

Love seeks only to uplift, to enlighten, to enable man to realize his inherent freedom. To render man whole and complete, untouched by disease, death, poverty, decay, discord – this is the intent of love. To bring harmony, peace, life, joy, enlightenment, strength and beauty to all is the purpose of its existence. All men who operate on a basis of Love will demonstrate this characteristic of edification.

Unconditional

The expression of Love is totally unconditional. It makes no demands, sets no pressures, creates no terms, establishes no provisions, obligations, stipulations or ultimatums. There are absolutely no strings attached in Love.

Truth-Seeking

Love seeks only the truth, the reality of existence, not in mortal terms but immortal ones. Not only does it seek truth, but it demonstrates it was well. Idle gossip and loose tongues propelled by foolish minds are totally antithetical to its Being. It does not recognize such behavior.

Patient

Love is the sanctuary of patience, the epitome of control. It does not hurry others, for it realizes that all things are successfully accomplished within the momentum of Divine speed. Love never complains because it knows that in the end it will always emerge triumphant.

Humble

It can never be said that Love is pompous, overly inflated and egotistical. Love desires no pomp and pageantry; it seeks no ostentation, quite to the contrary. Rather, it is quietly noble. Of itself, it is glory; it is majesty. It does not have to pretend or fabricate false or puffed-up images of itself, for it is whole, complete, unified.

Thoughtful

Indeed, Love is thoughtful, i.e., full of thought, especially in reference to the feelings and welfare of others. Love is not bound in a little shell overly concerned with its own self. Rather, it is boundless, radiant, omnipresent. Being thoughtful it is, therefore, considerate, i.e., it observes and is sensitive to the rights and feelings of others.

Equitable

Love is just; it is fair; it is always equitable. It treats all living things with reverence for life. It does not discriminate because of race, creed, color, religion, power, wealth, position or prestige. In Love's perspective all are equal and deserving.

Kind

Benevolent, charitable and gracious – these words typify kindness, whose nature it is to reach out, to give, to share. It is this kindness which is such a distinctive characteristic of Love, for when Love is expressed, there exists a quality of warmth, sincerity and compassion transcendent of all expression. Kindness is joy. It is the nobility of man being.

Imperturbable

Love is calm and steady, the antithesis of turbulence, always harmonious, never discordant. If aroused or provoked, it acts only in defiance of injustice, inequity, disease, limitation, mortality and all other atrocities which inhibit man from growing and realizing the majestic beauty of his divinity. This imperturbability is expressed as serenity, and he who is truly serene, who is Master, walks in and radiates an indomitable calm, a peace which quiets all inharmony.

Richard Andrew King

Generosity

Love gives, and he who has given – totally, completely, without thought of return – knows no greater joy. Giving is its own reward. Generosity should not be perceived as confining itself to money or things. The greater gifts are the fruits of the Spirit. The greatest gift of all is life – the vitality of existence, and the greatest gift of life is love. Both of these are given freely – the expression of God's generosity.

Completeness

Love is whole and complete, fully integrated within itself. It can never be jealous or envious, for the latter are manifestations of incompleteness. Jealousy and envy are founded on a fear of loss, either present or future, but Love realizes no loss. Therefore, it can never be incomplete.

Purity

This is one of the most challenging aspects of mastering Love. It confines itself not just to the cleanliness of body but, more importantly, to thought. Love maintains no thoughts of evil, malice, hate. Because it thinks no evil it expresses none.

Eternality

While many thoughts, things and actions are finite and ephemeral, Love is eternal. Furthermore, when other things fail and crumble under the weight of time, Love does not. It endures; it continues forever. It is this aspect of Love which makes it priceless. It is above all concept of cost. It can never be purchased, sold or traded. Hence, it is the most valuable of possessions. Other things may waste away but never Love. It may be placed on the shelf, even forgotten, but it is always in existence in unlimited supply, ready to be given form and meaning.

Strength

It may be contrary to popular opinion but Love is strong. In fact, it is the apotheosis of strength. Physical prowess has always been associated with power, but when Love is truly understood and demonstrated, there will be no equivocating as to what quality of existence is the epitome of power. When the brute force of the mortal wanes and dies and Love still remains intact and vital, as it always does, man will see and know that Love is strength in purest form.

Trusting

To love is to trust, to believe, to maintain faith, confidence, reliance in Truth. Trust is the foundation of real friendship, the adhesive force of every meaningful relationship.

These characteristics are a portion of all that Love is and even though their explanation only involves a few pages, the expression of them in an individual's experience should not be so diminutive. Love is, to be sure, a little four letter word, but it also is, to be sure, an experience of boundless majesty. It would be ineffectual to simply read about Love and not incorporate it into active life. Reading is good but the desired result is assimilation and demonstration.

Richard Andrew King

It should never be assumed that Love is an easy subject to master, especially at this level of existence. If it were, there would be more of it in expression than there currently is. It is the most difficult lesson the majority of us will ever have to learn. Yet, the greatest challenges also bring the greatest rewards, and because Love is the first priority it must also generate rewards of the first priority.

There are untold benefits to mastering the Love vibration but they will never be realized until the vibration is created and placed in motion. It is impossible to convey the joy which Love brings to the heart of the lover. It is also difficult to describe the peace, the calm, the beautiful serenity of Love or the sensation of the vibration which it generates. In fact, the only true way to realize these things is to love – sincerely, deeply, with conviction and purpose.

The challenge of mastering Love will be seen by each student when he realizes its magnitude and analyzes its individual parts. For example, Love thinks no evil thoughts. This includes the entire spectrum of negativity from envy to hatred. It means that Love is pure and good. Therefore, Love sees, thinks and interacts with others in relation to only one image – the perfect and divine. It cannot be hateful to others because it doesn't understand hatred nor spite, nor jealousy. It is totally unadulterated.

The challenge now begins to take form and meaning. How much thought is generated in the world today which is of this caliber of purity? How many minds can individually attest to being totally

The Karate Consciousness

free of all discordant and negative thought? How many minds perceive only the perfect, divine image in all people? How many are devoid of any forms of jealousy, envy, malicious desire and bitterness? How much mind power is given to the thought of all men being free, happy, abundant, healthy, successful, peaceful, alive, vital and whole? Love thinks and desires only these things, and the student who is to master Love must so discipline this aspect of his intellect that he identifies with and expresses the same.

Being of pure mind and thought is, of course, only one aspect of Love. Patience is another. How often does man, acting within the concept of mortality, lose control of himself either when alone or in the company of another or others? What percent of the time is man given to being in a hurry and working outside the limits of Divine Speed – the perfect momentum in which all things are accomplished?

Too, what of human pride and arrogance – those qualities which are the direct result of the Power in the Flock Syndrome? They are certainly no part of Love. Yet, they must be put aside if Love is to be genuinely expressed. With all of the emphasis placed upon extrinsic power today, this is certainly a lesson whose learning requires considerable effort.

This discussion could obviously continue. The point to be made is that Love is quite a challenge and a very important one at that. In fact, it is ineluctable for the aspiring consciousness.

Richard Andrew King

As this great lesson of Love is learned day by day, moment by moment, the individual will perceive a change in the quality of his life. It will increase noticeably. Many problems will automatically vanish. Personal health will increase, as well as attitude. Life will become more vital, interesting and meaningful. In all, the individual who loves will be whole, complete and functionally integrated. This he will call joy and he will be thankful for it as he moves ever closer to mastery of the life process.

FORGIVENESS

In keeping with the concept of individual completeness, the student should learn well the art of forgiveness. In order to be whole, spiritually integrated, it is necessary to relinquish all mortal propensities and perturbations. Resentment is one such characteristic. It is much like a chain or, in some cases a web of chains, which bind man to mortality, inhibiting his freedom to move and rise into the higher realms of consciousness. It is forgiveness which severs these inimical irons allowing for a natural ascension.

For example, if an individual feels he has wronged himself or been wronged by another and he lets himself be consumed by the inequity or injustice, his mind, continually focused on the problem, will not be free to channel its energies in more productive areas. Hence, he will be trapped. If he adds fuel to his resentment and it grows more intense, he is only weaving a web of enslavement. Trapped within his self-constructed prison walls, he will only suffer and remain diseased and discordant, a true slave of his own creation.

The way out of this precarious predicament, or the procedure to avoid it entirely, is, of course, through the art of forgiveness. To lay aside, to give up, to pardon, to let go of negative feelings completely is what forgiveness is all about. By utilizing forgiveness and, therefore, not incorporating hostility within the individual life framework, the mind is free to exist and rise in consciousness. There is no slavery because there is nothing to be a slave to.

The student of life will enhance his own growth and well-being if he learns to forgive himself and others of any wrong directed toward him. Within this learning process, he will see that forgiveness is a scientific principle of life, a law whose usage will bring harmony and peace to each person but which, more importantly, will allow him to be free, a condition absolutely essential to his continued edification.

Richard Andrew King

Destroy the bonds which chain you to the ground,
to the rock of mortal earth.

Sever the ropes of hatred, discord and disease and
leave them in the distant past to the artisans of
dissolution.

Cut the cord to all that straps you to the loadstone of
stagnation, and release resenting thought upon the
wings of ethereal wind.

Let go! Let Go! Let go and live!

Forgive!

THE ACCLAMATIONS

The manifestations of Love in society are deserving of recognition
and applause. Hence, they are referred to as "Acclamations."
Among them are esteem, respect, appreciation, acceptance,
gratitude, understanding and tolerance.

Esteem

It is natural and correct for every individual to view himself and
others with admiration. Regardless of previous teachings,
misdirected criticism and popular opinion, the student must see all

The Karate Consciousness

individuals as vital, necessary and important forces within the domain of creation. All are to be honored for their uniqueness, divine beauty and majesty. Everyone is an expression of the life force, and simply because of this they are deserving of approbation.

Respect and appreciation are related to esteem. The former is the realization and acknowledgement of the divinity within man. The latter is a sense of recognizing a continual increase in the value of each person.

Appreciate means to "increase in value or worth," just as its opposite, depreciation, means to "lower in value." Thus, as we appreciate all individuals, including ourselves, we are continually striving to see the good in all, good which does exist. The only difficulty is that often we must dissolve the imperfection which clouds our own understanding before we can perceive the good in others.

If we continually appreciate others, it stands to reason that we could never depreciate or deprecate them. This is why respect is of such importance in interpersonal and intrapersonal relationships (*interpersonal* is an individual's relationship with others, while *intrapersonal* is each person's relationship with his own Being). Appreciation always seeks the higher level. It is man's nature to want to be appreciated and, thus, when he is shown respect by being appreciated he responds positively.

Richard Andrew King

Respect, in its purest form, is not bound by qualification. Individuals should be respected simply because "they are." They exist. Whether we, in our limited perception, like it or not, all people spring from the same Source. They are made by the same Creator. Therefore, they are deserving of recognition and acknowledgement. White belt, black belt, no belt, president or pauper, young or old – it makes no difference. All are to be respected.

The Power in the Flock concept, however, would take the stand that only people who have power, position, prestige and/or money are respectable. Such is not the correct understanding. The biggest and the smallest, the richest and the poorest, the famous and the unknown, the educated and the illiterate – these, too, are respectable because of their divine origin and heritage.

Acceptance

This attribute is precisely what it signifies – being accepted, not rejected. Oftentimes, however, through ignorance, carelessness, or design, rejection is created. Perhaps there are times when it is appropriate. Yet, it should not be the norm. An overdose of rejection destroys the bonds between individuals and, hence, it is more difficult to build the kind of rapport needed to move the mass consciousness upward.

Acceptance is created through awareness of other people and the ability to see them as they are. This "acclamation," as the others, doesn't make qualifications because of money, prestige, position, external beauty, etc. It perceives the divinity within all men and accepts that.

Love is also manifested in society through gratitude, the condition of being sincerely thankful for others and their gifts. Indeed, there is great reason to be grateful for others because Love is paramountly expressed through people. No people, no expression of Love. Concomitantly, no realization of the joy and exhilaration which Love brings when given to others. How dull and vapid life would be without people and without their talents, abilities, intellects, senses of humor, laughter, warmth and the Love which they express. How uneventful it would be not to share the life experience of growing, learning, building, achieving, giving, etc., with others.

Man is divine, and part of his composition, even though it may be latent, is Love. He needs others to express Love, to give to them; to receive from them. People are, to be sure, a marvelous creation to be grateful for, not because they may give us things, but because they supply an outlet for us to give and, therefore, know the joy of giving, of loving.

Each individual will increase his ability to master the Love vibration as he generates and maintains a momentum of gratitude in relation to all things. Even periods of great tribulation are deserving of a grateful heart because they allow us the opportunity for becoming stronger, wiser, better. Individuals who have political, religious, economic or social viewpoints contrary to our own give us the chance to scrutinize our own beliefs and either change or corroborate them.

Adversity is the whetstone for sharpening the blades of our minds, wits and abilities. Even unjust criticism, attack or censure offers us a chance to develop the kind of character unscathed by such abuse. There is a reason to be grateful for everything, and the student should look for this reason continually in order to cultivate a consciousness of Love.

Understanding and tolerance are wonderful manifestations of Love. To be understanding is to comprehend, to grasp the meaning of things, conditions or people as they are. Tolerance is the capacity to endure them. How often is man intolerant of others while at the same time unconcerned with understanding them? How often is he intolerant of certain conditions or people which he understands completely? How often do people deny to others that which they demand for themselves?

Understanding requires the mental effort of perceiving what it is like to be in another's shoes, to have walked the same road he walked, experienced the same hardships and joys he did. Of course, such an understanding is difficult to obtain but being empathetic will help.

In the moment-to-moment exigencies of personal living it is often easy to forget that other people have problems, experiences and personal matters of their own. Thus, we become encased in a shell, centered in our own little worlds. Yet, the entirety of existence far exceeds our personal domain. Other people do exist "out there," and if we would become more understanding, we must expand our consciousness to this "outer space."

By focusing on the whole we will gradually increase our comprehension of it. We will become more understanding and, hence, our Love quotient will be enhanced.

As we become more understanding, we will also become more tolerant. It is often easier to endure other people, conditions and circumstances when we have a clearer picture of the whole. By being tolerant, friction and discordant vibrations will ease between people or between an individual and his psyche. Being so disposed, there is not such a propensity to change, criticize or proselytize, but simply to experience.

In spite of his personal feelings or attributes, each student of life must strive to be understanding and tolerant of himself and others. He cannot afford to dwell within the little domain of his own world and reject all else by being nonunderstanding because this attitude is restrictive, limiting, counter-productive and antithetical to the edification of the mass consciousness.

The Pinnacle

Perhaps the highest expression of Love is found in the word "caring." To care for all living things is a characteristic of the truly enlightened consciousness. To care for all is to care for life, the

Richard Andrew King

most precious gift and exultant joy of the universe. To care is to be concerned and interested. To care is to step outside of the shell; it is to cast a vote for life and its quality. To care is to live; to care is to truly love.

How magnificent our earth would be if "caring" for the welfare of all was the first priority? To what levels could mankind rise? What goals could he achieve? How far could he run? To what distances would the warmth of his love be felt? How many darkened corners of the universe would be illuminated if mankind of the planet earth were to genuinely care for all?

Such inquiries may seem only idealistic to some, dreams to others, but goals to those of Mind. Love is not just a word created to give majesty to thought. It is a principle of life to be demonstrably expressed by all for the ascending benefit of all. It is a challenge for the strong, the enlightened and the free. Love is caring, and it is the pinnacle of existence.

POTPOURRI

The Loving Male

Among the male populace there has existed, and still does exist, a belief that Love is a feminine characteristic to be expressed by the female only. Unfortunately, for the entire race, she alone has had to carry the flagstaff of Love in the greater proportion. Thus, the qualities of kindness, tenderness, gentleness, compassion and concern have been primarily associated with her.

The male can learn much about Love from his counterpart. Indeed, he must if the mass consciousness is to be elevated. It is not a belittling thing to love. It is the greatest of all things. The male needs to realize this for his own well-being. The reasoning that it is more natural for a woman to love because she bears the child in the womb and gives it birth is erroneous. Motherhood is, of course, only one-half of the picture. Fatherhood is as much a responsibility. Male and female both need to love. This is the way leading to harmony, to balance, to a perfect equilibrium of the life process.

The male, however, may find it difficult to love because of his suppression of Love in the past. Perhaps it could be argued that his involvement in the "hunt" and his responsibility of providing for the family has not allowed him the opportunity of sensitizing himself to the Love vibration. But the past is past. The times are no longer demanding of physical prowess. They demand sensitivity, understanding, feeling. Therefore, the male student of life should strive to become more sensitive and responsive. He has an infinite capacity to love, as all people do. Yet, he does need to exercise the functions of his heart and should to a greater degree. As he does this he will begin to truly understand what power there is in the great vibration, and he will see that Love is not a sign of weakness but the indelible mark of maturity, strength and wisdom.

Richard Andrew King

The Growth Spectrum

Love is the perfect medium for growth and learning. Its vibration is so harmonious that discord cannot exist. Thus, Divine Speed is established and the student can flow gracefully upward within the mainstream of his ascension.

In illustration of this, assume two individuals begin studying karate under different teachers. One instructor/pupil relationship is centered in Love; the other is not. The latter is characterized by indifference, fear, criticism, carelessness and a lack of reverence for life. The love-based relationship is just the opposite. Its characteristics are concern, caring, consideration, inspiration, warmth, strength and an unadulterated emphasis on life and edification. It is useless to ask which environment would be the most salutary for the student's well-being. Obviously, it is the love-based one, and the reason is quite simple. Man is divine. Love is a part of this divinity, and the student instinctively identifies with it because it is natural to him, to his true being of Oneness. Being natural, it is right. Thus, his growth is expedited and enhanced.

Cohesive Force

Love is the magnificent, cohesive force which holds the race of man together and enables it to reach into the skies of attainment and achievement. It is axiomatic that where there is no Love there is no bond – only separation and alienation. Sadly, the continuing divisive environment of the world in the first two decades of the Second Millennium and the 21st Century is demonstrative of an ever widening fissure among men and nations, thus betraying the divine majesty of love and its potential for the unification of man.

It is Love which unifies, for if the mass consciousness is to move upward as a whole, it must be precisely that, whole. If divided and separated, it can make no progress, just as a disassembled aircraft cannot fly. Love, however, is the uniting bond between people, the cohesive force which brings all men together as One and guarantees flight. With love there is hope. Without it only despair, discord and dissolution.

Artistry

Love is the greatest of arts; the mastering of the Love vibration pure artistry. Yet, any artisan will exclaim that to master an art requires study, practice and patience. It is not an accomplishment which can be achieved overnight.

And so it is with Love. It is the most demanding task. The novitiate Love artisan will probably find himself and his creations clumsy and awkward. The colors of his paintings may be dull and bland, the carvings of his sculpturing jagged and inordinate, the notes of his music rough and discordant, the movements of his dance sluggish and uncoordinated. Yet, with devout study, practice and an insatiable desire to succeed, his color will become vivid, his sculptured lines straight and smooth, his music melodious and his dance graceful and flowing. He will, in time, begin to create beauty and loveliness and eventually he will make

Richard Andrew King

the beautiful more beautiful and the lovely more lovely. He will then be a true artisan, a creator of divine resplendence.

Karateka, be an artisan of Love! Master its vibrations. Paint it across the heavens. Sing it continually. Create. Sculpture a universe of Love, and cast white radiance into the limitless boundary of infinity.

Love. This is the commandment. The directive cannot be more clear. Love is the outpouring of the heart. It is giving, sharing, caring, understanding, uplifting, being. It is the essence of life, the beauty of creation. Its power is indomitable. Indeed, the experiencing of the Love vibration is joy, splendor and unparalleled majesty. Seek it, student of life, for it is the divine radiance of the one who is Master.

Chapter 6

INDIVIDUALITY

Stand free and be, for you are but the exaltation of all
creation shouting to the wind.

You are the apotheosis of the Flame,
the radiance of the universe!

You are the magnificence of all that ever was,
or all that ever shall be.

You are life, love, peace, abundance, completeness
in Divine Design.

Richard Andrew King

You are hope, joy and inspiration,
the blessing and the gift of God.

Make no mistake. You are free!
And, furthermore, in answer to the Call –
Ageless, Deathless, Timeless and Immortal!

B e an individual! Rise to the apex of your identity. Stand courageously upon the towering precipice of time and proclaim with an indomitable spirit your right to grandeur and to greatness. Shout it to the wind if you must; whisper it in the silence; glorify it in your own soul, but do it. For the sake of freedom and the right to life for all men, for all time, stand free and be!

To truly be an individual is to be an artistic work of beauty, for individuality is the expression of man being centered in his own divine presence, and there exits no finer piece of artistry than this in all the universe.

The highest manifestation of such a functionally integrated soul is atonement. Its most exquisite vibration, Love. True individuality is not an intensification of the human ego. It is, rather, a level of conscious expression based in the realms of Spirit, the domain of God.

The Karate Consciousness

To be an individual is also to be self-reliant, to trust thyself; to stand amid the storm and the tempest with a calm resolve that all is well within the core of your Being. It is self-confidence, awareness, assurance. It is the ability to stand directly in the center of the turbulence and be at peace. Beset with a deluge of a thousand opposing forces, it is the individual who lifts his head with poise and radiates the presence of the power within.

REQUISITES

The demands of individuality are often quite strenuous, for a person must be willing to separate himself from the mass of humanity if his conscience or his growth requires it. This may take form as a physical separation or, perhaps, a social, political, religious or mental one. The separation has no limits. Family, friends, acquaintances – all may have to be placed aside if they are inhibiting and detrimental to individual growth.

This is not to say that such a separation must be effectuated for a person to be an individual. Individuality cannot necessarily be equated with separation. However, if it is needed, it must be made. To deny it when the inner voice supports it is a distinct violation of individuality. We must be willing to stand alone no matter what the consequences.

Richard Andrew King

Of course, such a total separation is the extreme rather than the rule. It is often unnecessary to effectuate such an act because most of the lessons to be learned in the continuum can be resolved within the realm of the individual consciousness. Not only can they but many should be. In fact, creating a separation may simply be an act of avoidance of a problem, not the solution of it. Sometimes, the only way is to stand and challenge the problem face to face.

Contrastingly, the solution to another problem may be the avoidance of it. For example, if a person is impatient with others, he cannot always avoid them because in doing so he will remain impatient. The correct solution would be to challenge the situation, learn and master the quality of patience. Yet, if an individual needs to learn about himself, who he really is within the core of his Being and he currently is centered in associations where other people are only concerned with externalities and have not as yet begun the majestic journey within, then the most viable solution would probably be to separate himself from such current associations in order to answer the beckoning call of his conscience.

Such a separation would be natural. We all grow at different speeds and have different lessons to learn in each life phase. Thus, each of us needs to understand and accept this. When we do, we will appreciate it when another person needs to place our company aside for his own well-being and vice versa. In such an understanding there is love. All exist for the welfare of all and

The Karate Consciousness

seek, in whatever way they can, to assist each person in the unfoldment and expansion of his individuality or divine identity.

One of the most significant requisites for individuality is the ability to think and act in accordance with the dictates of individual conscience. In other words, each of us must do what we feel is right, not what other people feel is right if, of course, we do not violate their rights and liberties.

This is not always as easily done as said. In today's society with the proliferation of various means of communication, such as television, radio, cell phones, the web and all of its technology, etc., certain messages or thoughts are easily spread throughout the mass consciousness. This latter instance may be dangerous to the principle of individuality but would only occur in a race of non-thinking automatons. Thus, as a people, we cannot afford to stop thinking or to relegate the thinking process to others. If we do this, we forfeit our right to individuality and create an atmosphere where slavery, limitation and restriction are only as distant as the emission of a thought, the push of a button or the click of a mouse.

The student of life must, therefore, learn to scrutinize and analyze his own thought. Are his beliefs the fabrications of other people, or are they the results of the operation of his own mental faculties? Is he doing what he truly wants to do, or is he responding to the desires of someone else? Are the thoughts of the mass consciousness congruent with his own or are they in contrast? Are his actions likewise predicated on external forces, or are they the

Richard Andrew King

direct result of internal creation? The true individual will always live within the dictates of his own conscience. Such dictates may be coincidental with others. The main criterion, however, is that they are generated internally, not externally. The admonition is: *Think and act in accordance with the dictates of individual conscience.* This is the true way to individuality.

WHY INDIVIDUALITY?

Perhaps it is absurd to ask, "Why individuality?" It may be that such a concept is already well-founded and well-expressed within the confines of planet earth. Or, it may be that there is such a lack of it that no one knows what it is or that they are completely comfortable with the concepts of conformity.

Whatever the stimulus behind the inquiries, there are definite reasons why individuality is an established principle and why it is a major lesson to learn in the life continuum. First, it is axiomatic that there is only one way to the higher plateaus of consciousness and that way is that each person must travel the road alone. There are no shortcuts, no bypasses and no free rides. All must make the journey by themselves. The process of spiritual ascent is a solitary climb, not a hand-holding exercise.

To some people this may be a startling revelation; to others, an established fact, but it is true. Certainly, we may meet friends along the way and even travel with them for a while, but no one can obviate or dissolve the obstacles which we must individually overcome. There is a divine plan and means of unfoldment for each person and no one can interfere with it.

It is by following the dictates of our own conscience that we coincide our energies with the divine plan intended for us and, thus, our upward progress is rendered perfectly efficient. By not being an individual, however, by attempting to live the lives of others or beckon to their desires, we remove ourselves from the flow of energy meant explicitly for us and inhibit our development.

Figuratively speaking, there is a groove, a stairway, a tube, a flight pattern all our own. It is the one most beneficial to our progress. Yet, if we're rolling along in someone else's groove, climbing their set of stairs or following their flight plan, we will be naturally detained. And we'll know it, too. If an individual is sincere about elevating his consciousness and traveling within the groove created just for him, all other paths will be discordant in varying degrees until he finds that one path in which all is harmonious for him. That path is the right one.

Secondly, it is the individual who is the universal basis of creativity. Bind him, destroy his identity, and he cannot create because he needs to be free to do so. Yet, give him the environment to express his individuality and he will create.

Richard Andrew King

What is created is another matter. However, as the understanding of the life force increases, as well as individual vibration, functional demonstrability will follow. The ensuing result will be beauty and loveliness, not only in things such as pictures, sculptures, works of art, etc., but also in attitudes, thoughts and personal relationships.

Thirdly, the times demand it. The world today needs true individuals – men and women of substance who are willing to promote and take a stand for the Divine, Perfect Man, not the imperfect, mortal one; individuals who live by high standards, who will not stoop to lesser ideals in order to placate others, prostitute themselves for thirty pieces of silver, compromise their beliefs for a minute piece of material comfort nor step on someone else simply to elevate their ego. Yes, "substance." This is the key word. Let us have individuals of substance, the hallmark of a new age.

> I AM was not created
> to live in the shadow of
> another man's dream,
> nor dwell in the distant reveries of
> another man's mind,
> but to stand in the light
> of his separate sun,
> illuminating the brilliance
> of his identity.

The Karate Consciousness

CROSSING THE THRESHOLD

To talk of individuality is easy. To live it is quite another matter. For most of us there exists a fear in facing the great I AM, a reluctance to shed the rags of social, religious, economic and political conformity and stand alone. To be different is potentially hazardous, for difference is often labeled "bad," and such a condition might create havoc in the flock, thus upsetting the status quo.

But difference is often what the flock needs for it to keep moving forward and progressing. As water which sits idle becomes stagnate, so does the mass consciousness when it idles away its time. There must be movement – a flow of mind power and related action if all is to be harmonious and continually beneficial.

It is each individual centered in his own Divine Presence which catalyzes the mass consciousness and enables it to move, to flow, to progress. Without true individuality there is stagnation – a state of affairs creating the environment for decay. Therefore, there must be souls willing to face the great I AM and overcome any fear necessary for its acquisition.

Cater not to the flock! Follow in the wing path of Jonathan Livingston Seagull who, having been evicted by the elders of his flock for daring to do what no other gull had ever done – achieve perfection in flight – rose to his divine identity, expressing his

Richard Andrew King

unlimited potential. Therefore, the rule is: cater to your own conscience, not to that of others! This is the admonition heralding the coming of each person's incandescent Dawn, the sunrise of eternal enlightenment establishing the apotheosis of one's true individuality.

In pursuit of this goal, be courageous! Be strong! Be resolute! Be indefatigable! Expand! Radiate! Obey the voice within! Follow it! This is the path to freedom, not just for one but for all.

WARNING SIGNALS

Perhaps the first mark of caution should be not to cast judgement on the flock as good or bad. It does have a consciousness all its own which, of course, is referred to as the mass consciousness. In other words, as a whole, it has an identity. Its emanations can be beneficial or destructive to individual growth, which brings us to the second warning signal: be careful of drawing your identity from the identity of the mass consciousness. If its understanding is greater than yours in some things it may be a valuable consideration to allow yourself the benefit of its knowledge and/or vibration. However, if you feel its understanding is lower than yours currently is, then by all means continue on the course of your growth because only you know what is instinctively beneficial to you, generally speaking.

"Generally" is used here because there do exist entities, i.e., living souls – be they individual or collective, who know what is better for us than we ourselves do. Yet, if there is a doubt as to whose judgement or understanding is the best in each particular case, then follow your own. This line of action may prove you right or wrong but at least you remain true to your conscience, which is the base line, the starting place for individuality.

The third warning signal is close to the second: if you must draw your identity, your strength, power, joy, peace, etc., exclusively from the flock, then it is most probably time you sat back and took cognizance of the situation and honestly evaluated your degree of individuality, for in all probability you are not your true self. You are probably somebody else's self.

True identity concentrates on knowing the Spirit which flows from within, and it takes all of its sustenance, peace, joy, strength, and so forth from the Source. Of itself, this Source is enough, and when an individual aligns himself with it he becomes whole, complete, unified, functionally integrated as a living Being.

What he knows within himself, he knows within others because he identifies with the Source residing in, sustaining and directing all people. He is strong and unafraid, knowing that his joy, peace and identity can never desert him. He is free. He can stand alone. He can stand amid the crowd. He can stand anywhere. It makes no difference where he is because at all times he is centered in the

Richard Andrew King

core of his Divine Presence, the great "I AM" – the spiritual edifice which forever remains unassailable and impregnable.

The forth caution is to know that in the quest for individuality there will be others who will lovingly assist you, some who will not care and others who will attempt to detain you. It is unfortunate that suppression of freedom and flight exists. It is not new. Jesus of Nazareth was subjected to it. Those people who were saturated with power in the flock feared him because the enlightenment he cast was too threatening to their cloistered dungeons of darkness. They mocked him, scorned him, attempted to destroy him. They could not because his consciousness had out-distanced mortality and all of its manifestations. Jesus was an exemplar of the Divine Identity.

However, Jesus has not been the only divine soul scorned by less evolved souls. Many Saints throughout history have had to bear the same type of hatefulness and antipathy, as well as their disciples. Saint Dadu Dayal (16th/17th Centuries) was persecuted for his teachings, as was Saint Ravidas (15th/16th Centuries), and Saint Dariya of Bihar (17th/18th Centuries).

The stimulus behind the suppression of freedom and individual progression is basically ignorance, an ignorance of Spirit, Mind, God.

Ignorance within the self will lead to self-suppression. Therefore, the student should acquire as much divine understanding as possible to prevent him from being his own worst enemy. Suppression from without is unfortunate but not as serious because nothing can really suppress or deny a consciousness centered in God. The real danger is in self-suppression as a result of personal ignorance.

A fifth warning signal is the concept of popularity. True individuality does not seek acclamation, acceptance or approval from the flock because in doing so it must relinquish or compromise its own beliefs and principles to fit those extraneous to its own. Thus, it may dissipate and weaken its composition and become "flock realized" as opposed to "self-realized." Not being true to himself, the popularity-conscious person will remain non-integrated and incomplete. His growth will not be enhanced and he will be precluded from obtaining the qualities of strength, joy and peace which can only come with wholeness.

Thus, in the pursuit or corroboration of individuality the student should learn to stand alone and remain recalcitrant to the whims of peer (flock) pressure. True, this is not always easy, nor sometimes even pleasant, but it is necessary. Know thyself; be true to thyself; be an individual.

A sixth cautionary sign is the belief that divine dispensation can flow through only one human being to another or others. For example, one person may convince a number of people that he alone can communicate and receive messages from the Almighty. All others must, therefore, follow him. The chain of command he establishes, if he has one, is the vehicle for transferring messages, and if the last person in the chain is to have any contact with his Creator, it must come though the chain.

This procedure is an efficient control strategy. By it, one person may have sole power over countless numbers of people. Yet, no one person, sect, religion or institution possesses a corner on the market of God or divine dispensation. As God is infinite, so are his methods of communication. Anyone can receive spiritual inspiration and guidance exclusive of another. The gifts flow more freely as individual consciousness is elevated but they are available to all. Many times it may be beneficial to have a personal teacher, guide, minister and so forth, but in the final analysis it is not necessary. One person, stranded, alone, in a universe of time and space would still maintain his divine relationship with God.

This is not to obviate the technique of establishing a hierarchy or chain of command to pass along the gifts of Divine Grace. Such lines of organization have proven their efficiency. What needs to be established is the idea that no mortal human being is sole recipient of God's love, life, knowledge, peace, inspiration, harmony, etc. All can receive. All can give.

The relationship between God and man is an individual personal matter, not a social one. Mind permeates all, not just a few who elevate themselves to the self-professed ranks of the chosen or elect. It is not for one to make decisions salutary to the well-being of all. Each individual is ultimately responsible for himself. He must, therefore, look to himself – to his God Presence within, not the mortal presence without, to find the correct knowledge relative to his unfoldment. Thus, the student should appreciate a hierarchy or chain of command for its merits but understand that nothing can supersede his individual contact with his Creator.

The final warning signal is the realization that no man is really an island, for all comprise the sea of life. As a collective body, we are a brotherhood of individuals, not a colony of isolationists inclusive of all planetary bodies and planes of existence within the universe. Regardless of all theories of duality or triality ad infinitum, we are One. The goal, however, is to enhance this Oneness and make it a creation of resplendent beauty. It is an exquisite goal, and its achievement will be exasperatingly radiant.

In reference to creating beauty for all, we must begin with ourselves as single units, take what we have and refine it. Our whole beings – including our attitudes, mannerisms and treatment of all living things, should not be rough, discordant, crude, primitive, vitriolic, deprecating and insensitive but smooth, harmonious, loving, sensitive and inspirational. We should be liquid essence, ever flowing warmly and gently through the corridoes of life. Such a status will result, of course, with mastery of the Love vibration – the highest manifestation of individuality.

Richard Andrew King

BEARER OF THE FLAME

The individual, rightly standing in the center of his Divine Presence, is, unequivocally, the bearer of the flame of life and freedom. He is inspiration, and through him life is revitalized, energized. Thus, to destroy individuality is to deny life; it is to place bonds and shackles on the concept of freedom. In understanding this, dear student of life, recognize and applaud individuality wherever it may be. Promote it. Support it. corroborate it. And, by all means, demonstrate it – moment to moment, hour by hour, day by day, year by year, life phase by life phase. It is a great blessing and one of the most salient lessons to be learned in the continuum.

Chapter 7

PURITY

The expression of Divine Perfection is facilitated through non-adulteration of the life system. In other words, the three components comprising individual Being – physical, mental and spiritual, must be as pure as possible in order to conduct the energy, intelligence and substance of God freely and efficiently. Any stoppages in the system will inhibit, if not preclude, the natural flow of these emanations and create an impasse to the achievement of the Divine Identity.

As we grow within the continuum, our goal is to keep the components of body, mind and spirit free of refuse and debris so the entire system is as clear a transparency as possible for the

Richard Andrew King

transmittal of light and life-giving forces. To obtain this freedom we need to be purification-conscious and subsequently follow the directives generated by such a state of being.

Purification and, more explicitly the word "purity," have come under great attack in today's contemporary world. To be "pure" is to be outdated, or so this belief contends. However, purity has never been more in style as far as the emerging and expanding consciousness is concerned. There is no need to deprecate nor to be iconoclastic. The time is always *now* and the demands of life must be met within the ever-present present.

THE ANALOGIES

Assume you are an automobile or any mechanical device for that matter. For you to be one-hundred percent efficient, all of your working parts must be clean, well-lubricated, free of defects and synchronized with each other. If there is dirt or debris in the system, it will not run or, if it does run, it will do so in varying degrees of inefficiency depending, of course, upon the severity of the complication. Your automotive system must be pure for you to be functionally operative.

Now assume you are a bar of gold. Your value in the market places of the world will be determined by your purity. If contaminated with foreign substances, your worth will be lessened in relation to another like bar of gold totally free of all impurities. Purity does have intrinsic value.

Third analogy. You are a particle of water. In your free state your ability to vibrate is extremely high. Electrical currents are facilitated by your Being. But if you allow yourself to be absorbed by substances which do not conduct electricity, your vibration quotient will be drastically lessened. You will not be able to avail yourself of higher energy sources.

The final analogy is that you are a pane of glass. If you are clean and transparent, you can conduct light extremely well. If, however, you are covered with materials which do not allow for the free passage of light, your transparency will be negatively affected, even opaque. By your nature you will not be an instrument for the passage of light.

All of the foregoing analogies are applicable to our life systems. For us to be efficient, well-functioning entities, the various components of our Being – physical, mental and spiritual, must be in the best possible working order. The substances of which we are comprised must, like pure gold, be unadulterated. They must also be, like water, conducive to the flow of energy and, as clear glass, transparent in order to facilitate the passage of light. It is no matter involving philosophical contemplation to be purification conscious. It is scientific fact. In order to rise to ever-increasing states of consciousness and move toward the attainment of Divine Perfection, purity is obligatory.

Richard Andrew King

THE COMPONENTS – PHYSICAL

The physical body is a blessing. As a vehicle, it transports and facilitates our movement in this plane of existence. In the light of our current condition it is a necessity and has, of course, been poetically referred to as the "Temple of the Soul."

Divine admonitions require that we do not neglect or abuse this temple. The reality of it in our existence is not a right but a privilege, and in order to sustain it we must assume responsibility for its care. To neglect it is to neglect the whole of our Being and jeopardize the possibility of obtaining an increased status of existence.

In relation to the physical aspect of our life system, one of the first remedies which comes to mind to avoid system stoppages is exercise. Indeed, this has merit. The underlying reason for physical activity is that it keeps the flow of living substance in perpetual motion. Water, oxygen, nutrients, etc., are carried in the blood to nourish every part of the body. More importantly, however, the composite of energy, which we are, is also kept in motion. It remains vital, moving, dynamic. It is this energy with which we must be primarily concerned because more than blood, water, oxygen, a host of elements and so forth, we are entities of intelligent, centralized, amalgamated, divine energy. Thus, in order to perpetuate life, we must keep this energy in motion; insure that it is alive and dynamic.

By not remaining physically, mentally and spiritually active, we deny this energy an avenue for expression. It slows down and we slow down accordingly by natural law. We lose vitality and energy because we put the brakes on our own flow of divine energy. Thus, we get run-down and tired, not because we have no energy but because we have shut it off and curtailed its perfect flow.

This certainly does not obviate our requirement for daily rest, but it does obviate an excessive amount of rest during our waking hours. Our whole Beings must be charged with energy, and we must charge them. Physically, mentally and spiritually we must be aggressively active, not overly fast or sluggishly slow, but moving at a perfect speed. And this speed is not difficult to determine either if we are tuned into our divine presence. Perfect speed is always harmonious. If our flight is too swift or too slow we will instinctively know it because when man is "at one" with his Creator it is virtually impossible to express any other quality than perfection.

Karate is an excellent vehicle for physical activity. It offers a myriad of exercises for the entire body, and it can also be a social or individual engagement depending upon personal disposition. It also has functional significance as a means of self-defense in the physical realm but, too, it offers a unique educational avenue for learning and expressing principles of life, love, peace, balance, control, confidence, focus and concentration, flexibility of mind and body, coordination, creativity, humility, strength, courage, wisdom and understanding.

Richard Andrew King

Physical exercise, as anything, can be carried to extremes. An excess of anything, as a general rule, is not conducive to individual well-being because excesses create an imbalance in the life system, and just as it is impossible to walk a straight line when out of balance, it is equally impossible to advance in consciousness when there is no stability. The age-old concept of "moderation" is, therefore, applicable to physical exertion as it is in all things. This moderation, though, must be tailored to each person as he follows the blueprint for his own unfoldment. No individual should claim another's degree of moderation as his own because growth is an individual activity within the divine consciousness, and the garments of individuality are always tailor made.

Physical exercise is not, of course, the only means of preventing life-system stoppages, and thereby assuring a continual, even flow of energy. Dietary measures should also be considered. Again, the concept is balance. Too much of one kind of food, too little of another, or the absence of another is incongruent with principles of health.

It is interesting that in today's world the discussion of what constitutes good dietary habits is ever-unfolding. As something new is discovered, the old is often laid aside. This is progress. Yet, contemporary man doesn't have all the answers relative to the most salient dietary formulas. Therefore, the student of life should act upon his own knowledge derived from informed sources, as well as his own experience and intuition in determining what is best for him.

Two principles to be noted in this matter are balance and flexibility. The latter is necessary from a growth standpoint, for if a food substance is proven salutary or detrimental to personal health, the individual should have the flexibility to either abandon the old or support the new. To remain recalcitrant to the indomitable principle of change and its manifestations is to pursue a course leading to atrophy and stagnation.

The usage of drugs and alcohol in today's society is alarming because such substances, consumed in excessive or even moderate quantifies, have proven their detriment. Man, as he stands within the core of his Divine Presence, is perfect. He is creation, life, harmony, joy, peace, love and light. He doesn't need chemicals or substances to pump him up, calm him down, hallucinate his mind, excite his imagination or creativity. The entire spectrum of universal experience is at his command if he will only awaken to this realization. And awaken he must, for the utilization of such substances is poisonous to the unfoldment of his perfection.

The whole process of ingestion and assimilation of toxic imbalancing substances is an escape from reality, a means of avoiding the tests and challenges requisite for individual growth. Such an escape may be the result of unknowing, uncertainty, misinformation, misdirected intentions, fear, or even a lack of courage in coming to grips with the truth. But for whatever reason, the escape is always an escape, not a conquest or victory.

Escapism, while generating temporal satisfaction, also compounds the problems which motivate the individual to seek such a release in the the first place. The only solution is to stand and fight each problem face to face. There may be initial failure, but as long as the heart is willing and impregnable, courage and understanding will be acquired in the struggle until sufficient quantity is obtained to overcome the obstacle at hand. Students of life, denounce and forego the usage of debilitating substances. They are chains and shackles, enemies to your highest good.

THE COMPONENTS – MENTAL

Two of the least recognized considerations given to the life-purification process are the creations and emanations of the mind. Yet, these elements are vitally important. It is incongruent with the principles of divine flow to simply concentrate on the physical and neglect the mental or spiritual. All of these parts coalesce to form one, unified, whole, functionally integrated individual. Therefore, all must be considered and given the appropriate attention.

For example, a person may take excellent care of his physical body – exercise it, give it the proper nourishment, keep it clean, but engage in such mental acts that his mind remains impure or stagnate. The effect this has on his entire Being is prohibitive to growth and the elevation of consciousness.

The mind is like a filter. As long as it's clean and well-maintained it will keep the system running smoothly, but if allowed to clog up and fall into disrepair, system stoppages will occur. As the body, the mind must be kept free of impurities.

The debris which creates system impasses in the mental component, which retards and defiles man, is an assortment of ruinous, incendiary, low-frequency, poisonous thought patterns and emanations. Following is an introductory list of these mental cancers.

LIMITATION

The words and phrases, *I can't*, *it's impossible*, *I give up*, *I'm nothing*, etc., are self-generated shackles of imprisonment. They are, perhaps, the greatest detriment to freedom and beautiful living. How can man grow, elevate his consciousness and increase his vibration when his own thought precludes these activities? How can he stand alone and be free when he denies himself and those concepts which are the door to his freedom? Obviously, he cannot. He will always be bound to the plains of captivity until he clears his mind of such deleterious atrocities. The life system must *flow* and the only way to keep it going is to functionally adopt the principles of non-limitation, possibility and divinity.

Richard Andrew King

The beauty of life is flight. Therefore, student of life, fly! Be! You always can and you always will do anything you desire if you saturate yourself in possibility. Yours is not the earth, it is the universe and everything beyond. Seek it and radiate the magnificence of your Being!

LUST

Lust is excessive, superfluous, unrestrained desire. It's applicable to many things but in all cases is prohibitive to growth because it establishes an imbalance in the life system and in some cases totally blinds individual perception of the macrocosm. Lust creates tunnel vision because the individual affected by it focuses his attention on one thing and thereby becomes oblivious to the entirety of his environment inclusive of financial, emotional, intellectual, physical, spiritual, social, religious, scientific, philosophical, marital and recreational aspects.

However, in order for man to make progress in the attainment and expression of his divine identity, he must be whole and totally in balance. The imbalance created by lust deters the individual from being whole, and his chances of realizing his divinity are correspondingly precluded.

As part of his training, the karateka must learn physical balance in order to effectuate specific movements and increase his artistic ability. It is the concept of balance which he must transfer from the training arena to his personal life, knowing that as he attains more balance in his life he will increase the quality of it.

The lust for money, prestige, power in the flock, food and sex are five of the major factors creating imbalance in the life system, i.e., they are system stoppages. If advocated or expressed by the majority of people they create the mass consciousness and, thus, as a whole, the society is imbalanced and its growth and spiritual evolution proscribed.

Needless to say, lust has to be nonexistent if the life stream is to flow uninterruptedly. This will only occur when the understanding is reached wherein the importance of balance and completeness are more important in creating beautiful life expressions than money, flock power, prestige, food or sex.

Lust is quite identifiable with the human, not divine, condition. To nullify its momentum requires discipline, and it is this factor which the karateka should learn and transfer to the everyday movement of his life in order to remove lust from his life stream. Once it becomes nonexistent, the individual will realize greater freedom, and he will move more rapidly toward his residence on the plains of joy.

Richard Andrew King

Yours is not the earth,

it is the universe and everything beyond.

It is the sky which lies beyond

the realms of distance run.

It is the light which radiates

from a live, yet unknown sun.

It is the sea which rolls and roars

in another universe and time.

It is the undiscovered passages

and corridors of Mind.

This is your domain and it is all –

all that ever was, that is,

and all that ever is to be.

Expand your consciousness, my friend

and bathe it in eternity.

NEGATIVE PATTERNS

Other system stoppages initiated through mental faculties are negative thought structures such as fear, criticism, worry, anxiety, self-centeredness, condemnation, intolerance, prejudice, hatred, envy, greed, poverty, revenge and animosity. These are all created and nourished in the mind. Hence, they can be dissolved and eradicated from experience by internal, mental control.

Admittedly, this is not easy but that does not preclude its necessity in creating a purified life system. It requires discipline, control, concentration, the ability to bring into reality the patterns established mentally, courage, as well as a fervent desire to be a truly integrated, whole, compete person, catalyzed by an enlightened understanding.

As each negative pattern is excised from individual consciousness, there will gradually emerge a sense of loveliness, a feeling of peace and solidarity unknown to states of discord. This is the natural warmth intrinsic to the divine consciousness. It is, for all intents and purposes, inexplicable and ineffable. Yet, it does exist and it is that lush, green meadow where the soul can live, breathe and create in a panoply of resplendent sunshine – a substantial reward for the purification of the mind.

THE COMPONENTS – SPIRITUAL

The spiritual demands for purification can, perhaps, best be associated with three words: life, love, light. The last of these, light, is not only the symbolic representation for wisdom, knowledge and understanding, but also a very real and radiant emanation from the body as individual consciousness centers itself in the core of Mind and God; thereby establishing Oneness.

Spiritual purification for mortal man, simply stated, is a return to a realignment with the Source. It is the ascension of man to God, as one not separate from but congruent with God. The requirement for spiritual purification is that we shed the garments of mortality and acquire the clothing of immortality, i.e., we surrender the finite self, which merely survives in a world of external illusion, and corroborate the infinite self which lives, grows and radiates within the nucleus of internal reality.

The great underlying principle which makes it possible to eventually return to the Source is integrity. It is strength. It is power. It is a spiritually scientific factor in the purification process.

An individual who embodies integrity is complete, and being so integrated he has no need of drawing from others to substantiate his true worth. The thoughts and related acts of prevarication, falsification, improper fabrication and unlawful appropriation are major violations of integrity – the keynote of a truly integrated individual.

The intrinsic value of integrity cannot be underestimated, for it is the epitome of truth, and truth is the only way to an enlightened and elevated consciousness. Forsake the assimilation and expression of integrity and honesty in the life stream and the possibility for attaining divine perfection might as well be cast into the abyss of oblivion.

Working within the concept of cause and effect, if we are truthful then, as we pursue it, the truth of our existence will flow to us as a

The Karate Consciousness

matter of natural law. However, the reverse is also true – ignore truth and it will evade us. Fortunately or unfortunately, therefore, our attainment is dependent upon certain rules, and if we would succeed, we must play by them. Unlike the conventions of mortality, there is no stretching of rules or cheating in the game of life edification. All is in perfect response to definite, precise, totally equitable, perfect Law.

As blood is the medium through which the body receives oxygen, water, nutrients, vitamins, etc., so truth is the medium for divine dispensation. Deny truth and the flow of spiritual nutrients ceases. Such a denial is committed when a person takes something from someone else, no matter how small, and without permission, or when an individual acts contrary to his conscience or when he deliberately avoids the truth.

The student of life should test this law and prove for himself that integrity is, indeed, power. But in the process he should not compare apples with oranges. Certainly, disembarking from truth may gain power in the flock and expedite an individual's ascension to high places within the mortal spectrum, but to achieve real internal power, well-established in the framework of immortality, is another matter. It is the one deserving of consideration.

Richard Andrew King

IN SUMMARY

This chapter has given a brief overview of the purification process. To be sure, it is absolutely essential that the total life system, inclusive of physical, mental and spiritual components, be continually purified if the student is to achieve the hallmark of divine perfection. This demands moment-to-moment concentration in thought and action.

The individual should find this task ineluctable. It is not a process which can be completed overnight because it is as infinite as the life stream itself. The objective is to create a consciousness which is nothing more than a transparency for the pure and unobstructed passage of the Light. This is the glory of living and the acknowledged trademark of a Mystic Master.

Chapter 8

THE D. C. FACTOR

The expression of Divine Perfection can only be realized through self-mastery. The surrender of the speciously authentic external self to the absolute and eternal internal self; the ability to direct and maximize the flow of universal energy as it relates to individual Being, the power to create and enhance life, the expressed capability of love, and the unprecedented talent of Light emission are all the resultant manifestations of the Master's touch. Mastery is the open door to attainment. But the trick is to get the door open so attainment may be realized. This is where the *D.C. Factor* is utilized.

Richard Andrew King

"D" and "C" are the initials for *Discipline* and *Control* respectively. Thus, we have the *Discipline-Control Factor*. This idea is basic to all principles of achievement, for without it there could be no continued accomplishment.

The relationship between Discipline and Control is that the former generates the latter. Control is regulation. Discipline is the training and exercise needed to effect the regulation. In karate, for instance, the placement, power and effect of any striking blow, be it a kick, punch, chop, rake, thrust, etc., is variable. Proficiency, however, and the extent of the variations is a matter of control. Yet, as any practitioner will confirm, the achievement of control takes work, concentrated effort, practice and repetition. Discipline is the force which binds all of these components together and creates the efficiency.

If there is any trait or characteristic of mastery in anything, it is control. The successful painter, musician, ballerina, writer, architect, athlete, business executive, public speaker, educator, pilot, etc., all express control in their work because without it there would be chaos and disorder. Success is the result of the ability to control. To be clear: control is the mark of a master.

In achieving self-mastery, therefore, we must learn to control ourselves, our actions, our thoughts. But in this lesson of learning control, we must also subject ourselves to discipline. This facet of living is generally the most disliked. It's fun to be in control, to so move the strings of the lyre that only beautiful, mellifluous melodies are created, but it's not so fun to subject our hearts, minds, souls and bodies to the discipline, the long tedious hours of practice, the sweat, the pain, and the agony required to produce beautiful music and artistry.

Mastery – all of its manifestations, joys and exhilarations – has its price. But in order to cross the bridge to this realm of ascendancy we must pay the toll. It is not so great an expense, although many consider it an exorbitant fee. But regardless of the price, the fields of perfection are the most exquisite gardens of beauty, and many enlightened souls are expending their last pieces of silver to cross to the other side.

The D.C. Factor – Chronology

Discipline ➡ Control ➡ Mastery ➡ Perfection

THE IMPOSITIONS

Basically, there are two ways to impose discipline: intrinsically (self-imposed) and extrinsically (non-self-imposed). The former is the higher ideal and should be strived for and maintained by the student. The latter may be considered as the ladder to the former. Non-self-imposed discipline is when others provide the regulation we need in order to progress.

Richard Andrew King

Regardless of how it is achieved, a high degree of discipline is essential to a well-functioning life system, for it is always the discipline that insures control, and it is control that effectuates transition to increased levels of expression of the life force.

The advanced karateka knows full well the importance of the D.C. Factor. It is the only way to attainment in the art. In the incipient stages of his training, he receives non-self-imposed discipline from his instructor in the teaching session. During individual practice he utilizes self-discipline. As he progresses along the vertical growth spectrum, the amount of discipline should shift gradually from the extrinsic to the intrinsic form, for the goal is to reach a state of total, individual integration, part of which is self-discipline. The new student should welcome this concept of discipline, for as he learns it he can transfer its principles to other areas, employ them in his daily experiences and increase the quality of his life.

When we speak of discipline in either form we are not referring to harsh criticism or censure but guidance and positive regulation. We all need discipline, and as we utilize it to refine and polish ourselves and our abilities, we must be careful to do it in a loving manner with care and concern. If self-imposed, love may be assured. However, if we are the recipients of extrinsic discipline, we can only hope that love is the dispensing agent. In the latter case, even if there is little love rendered, wisdom dictates that we acknowledge what is meant for our well-being and forgive the disciplinarian for any absence of the great vibration. However, it

The Karate Consciousness

must not be overlooked that discipline can be a form of love and this needs to be considered when evaluating any disciplinary measures.

THE STAIRWAY

Discipline and control, as other lessons in the continuum, come in stages with each successive step being dependent upon the preceding one. For example, a karateka needs to master a snap kick before mastering a snap-roundhouse kick combination and so forth. The idea is to begin with a relatively easy task, accomplish it, generate a successful attempt and a feeling of confidence and then exercise a larger amount of discipline, a newly acquired degree of control, and proceed to a more difficult task, generating more success, more confidence, etc., ad infinitum. It's just like climbing up a stairway. The "spinoff" is always an increased amount of self-assurance and self-reliance. Too, the quantities of discipline and confidence are continually enhanced. In fact, they may not even be noticeable until the student pauses and looks behind to see how far he has actually progressed.

One main caution here, however, is that the student shouldn't try to express the degree of discipline and control of the fortieth step on the stairway when he realistically has only enough to presently reach the sixteenth step. All will come in time. By imposing unrealistic abilities on his psyche, he will only become frustrated and run the unfortunate risk of defeat – a state of affairs which can

Richard Andrew King

be avoided if patience, wisdom and understanding are employed. All is perfect in Divine Speed. Success cannot be avoided if the desire for it is sincere and the heart and mind are unrelenting in its pursuit.

MORNING REINS

The most efficacious time for the inculcation of the D.C. Factor is in an individual's formative years. Generally speaking, at the current level of enlightenment of the mass consciousness, this means childhood. When a growing youth learns discipline and control, he can deal much better with problems, adversities and other various circumstances of life in the stages of adulthood.

However, a warning should be given here because, in the true concept of the continuum, age is meaningless. An individual's "formative years" are infinite. They are not really confined to that period of life between birth and age eighteen, twenty-one, etc., because as a person is growing, expanding his mind and elevating his consciousness, he is always formulating new ideas, concepts and ideals. A person's formative years may begin at seventy-two, eighty-four or ninety-nine. Life is eternal growth, and there is no limit as to when it can begin or end. Thus, the student will be much better off if he considers himself as ageless – not as a person who is X number of years old – but as an individual unbound by age and limitation, a living soul in infinite progression.

> Patience – the virtue,
> brings All to those
> who wait, who struggle,
> who persevere.

THE INDOMITABLE CALM

The direct manifestation of discipline and control is an indomitable Calm, a sense of peace, serenity and tranquility impregnable by any vibration of discord. More precisely, this Calm is really unreachable by discord because the vibration which accompanies this Calm is much higher than those of dissonance. The peace so far exceeds the turbulence that it can't be touched by it.

We are speaking of the ideal, of course. In the quest for this status, i.e., before the ideal is obtained, there will be moments when a minor degree of calm may be brought into some turbulence. However, as the student continually monitors his thoughts and actions and cultivates the Calm while dissipating the discord, the gap will widen until that moment is reached when he will have moved himself completely out of range of all negative, disturbing vibrations. He will, therefore, have arrived at that characteristic of his countenance known as the *Indomitable Calm*.

Richard Andrew King

In relation to this Calm, the principles of balance, poise, harmony and peace must be mentioned because they are intrinsic to it. The achievement of balance is one of the major stepping stones to the Calm because it is, indeed, an effect of control. Anyone who has ever tried to stand on one foot, any gymnast who has mastered a handstand, any karateka who has executed a snap kick-side knife thrust kick-rear kick combination all in one flowing movement will testify to the importance of balance in the successful accomplishment of each maneuver.

The previous examples encompass the physical realm, although balance is principally an activity of the mind, i.e., it is the mind which instructs the body. Yet, balance, as a concept of living, should not be limited to the aspect of our physical or mental natures only. It is the components of the life system – physical, mental, spiritual – all in "balance" together which result in a highly efficient expression of the life force.

Poise, it may be argued, is the artistic manifestation of balance. Poise is composure, equanimity, that beautiful characteristic which stands unyielding to tempestuous winds. Part of the essence of karate is to generate this artistry of poise, to elevate the consciousness so it stands straight, erect and dynamically powerful – an edifice of august splendor.

Poise is not arrogance or a haughty display of the little self. Rather, it is a knowing, an intuitive, percipient understanding of divine individual presence. When an individual stands truly poised he stands in the center of God. With His omnipotence and omnipresence there is genuine stature, the word for which is *poise*. Harmony and peace may be considered as synonyms for the Indomitable Calm. Where the Calm exists, there will always be harmony and peace and vice versa. None can exist without the other.

Harmony is sweet accord. Peace is blissful serenity. In harmony all things occur in clockwork precision. In peace all movement flows smoothly to divine rhythm. The statutes of divinity demand the harmonious, the peaceful, the poised and the balanced. The loving admonition for every student of life is to align the centers of heart, soul, mind and body so that only these qualities are emitted from the life system. Therefore, dear student, seek to be the *Indomitable Calm*.

When confronted with negative,
discordant vibrations,
let not your peace become
one with the violence.
Rather, let the violence become
one with your peace.

Richard Andrew King

STRESS

Stress is pressure, strain, accentuated force. It is often considered diabolically inimical to individual well-being. Perhaps. However, stress and the adversities which accompany it are one of the most salient assets in the elevation of individual consciousness. Stress and adversity should, therefore, be perceived as blessings, not anathemas.

Why such a perception? Because when, through discipline, we learn to control increasing degrees of stress, we automatically move higher in our functional demonstrability of the life force. In other words, we have met and conquered and taken one more step along the road to mastery.

How could we possibly progress without stress, adversity, obstacles and challenges of increased dimension? How can we hope to move higher in our consciousness if there is nothing placed before our minds and hearts to test us and, thereby, prove our ability to radiate at increased vibratory levels? How could we know victory if there were no races to win? How could we learn to master the sea if there were no storms and tempests to sharpen, refine and increase our sailing abilities and knowledge? How could we know what it's like to be elevated if there were no mountains to climb? And how could we ever know what it is to be a diamond glittering in the crystalline beauty of the Light if there were no pressure to coalesce our molecules into the radiant form of resplendence?

Obviously, these are rhetorical questions because each of us knows, consciously or unconsciously, that if we are to progress, we must be tested again and again if need be before we emerge victorious and move forever higher within the avenues of the continuum.

Karate, as a developmental system, places increasingly greater amounts of stress on the student as he strives to move higher in his expression of the art. Exercises become more difficult and involved; kata and kumite techniques are more intricate. Thus, he is continually challenged with new adversities, new obstacles, new barriers to overcome. As he surpasses them, he gains confidence and, hopefully, an increased understanding of his own illimitability. But in order to surpass each new obstacle, he is required to exercise greater discipline, greater control. Such is the process of his unfoldment.

The experience of daily living also provides a multifarious array of stress factors. These may be generated by the rapid pace of living usually found in metropolitan cities; business pressures; differences in personalities; economic, social, political, environmental problems, etc. The key is not to allow these "stress situations" to render the individual distressed but, when and if they arise, to utilize them to acquire more self-restraint and control.

Richard Andrew King

168

The technique to effect such a condition is to use the force of the stress to act as the catalyst to produce the Calm. This is simply a mental process. As stress occurs, the individual relaxes, goes within and establishes an impregnable sense of tranquility. As he exudes peace, he cannot be distressed. True, this does require discipline, but when the student learns to control such circumstances, he will realize a loveliness of life never before known.

The experienced karateka understands this principle. For example, if he is physically pushed to the ground, he is trained to instantaneously relax and roll as he falls. The first is to alleviate the possibility of damage caused by rigidity; the second is to redirect the flow of energy in a beneficial direction rather than contribute to its abrupt, jolting termination upon impact – an action which could produce rather serious injuries.

This type of strategy may also be useful in making the most of any stress situation. Relax, roll and redirect the forces of adversity rather than meet them head on. Discord and dis-ease occur when there is tension, rigidity and turbulence, so to keep the life system running smoothly, simply relax and flow.

When the student can meet great turbulence with great calm, he is well on his way to mastery. When he can totally annihilate the turbulence with his Calm, he will be Master, the end result and manifest application of the D.C. Factor.

The Karate Consciousness

To this end, one of the primary sayings of the Karate Institute of America that every student learns is this:

Diamonds are made under extreme heat and pressure over an extended period of time; not by a mere and casual blowing of an intermittent wind.

Very simply, if the practitioner of karate, as well as life, desires to be a diamond rather than a common chunk of coal, he needs to embrace the heat, pressure and time involved in becoming such a valuable and sparkling gem. Chunks of coal are common. Diamonds are not. For each of us to rise to the level of excellence in anything we must be willing to accept the challenges and opportunities that stress blesses us with. Yes, blesses us, for without stress how could we be challenged to reach new heights of attainment?

Here's an excellent quotation regarding stress from Great Britain's extraordinary 20th Century leader Sir Winston Churchill:

Kites rise highest against the wind, not with it.

From Kahlil Gibran, the famous Lebanese-America poet, we read:

Out of suffering have emerged the strongest souls. The most massive characters are seared with scars.

Richard Andrew King

World renowned Helen Keller shares this truth:

Character cannot be developed in ease and quiet.
Only through experience of trial and suffering can the
soul be strengthened, ambition inspired, and success achieved.

THE THOUGHT GAUNTLET

As each individual Being passes through the continuum, one of the greatest challenges of the D.C. Factor is posed by the *Thought Gauntlet*. The most popular meaning of a gauntlet is a double file of people, usually armed with some kind of weapon, through which, for whatever reason, another person or persons must pass. The object, of course, is for the participant to make it successfully from one end of the gauntlet to the other without crumbling under the blows of those who form the file.

Our whole mortal thought processes may be likened to this idea of a gauntlet because the emanations of our mental faculties often are our greatest adversaries in the movement from mortality to immortality. In themselves they can beat us to the ground, cripple us and, thereby, detain our success.

Our ability to exercise discipline and control, however, offers a formidable weapon against the *Thought Gauntlet*. Unless we can discipline our minds to control our thoughts, we will have little chance to effectuate mastery and reach the realm of Perfection.

The Karate Consciousness

We are what we think, and if this statement is sincerely and intensely cogitated upon, the cataclysmic importance of individual thought regulation will rise plainly into view.

Mental discipline is more subtle than physical. We can watch the body and its movements as it is subjected to the D.C. Factor, but that of the mind is not so readily perceptible. We cannot see thoughts, although we may feel them and witness their effects. Hence, it's more difficult to effect regulation. Nonetheless, regulation may be imposed. It is simply more demanding.

A meaningful exercise in mental discipline is the continual perception of each individual as a perfect, pure and radiant creation of the life force. In other words, when each of us looks at another person, do we see that person cloaked in mortality, a heart of bitterness and anger, a mind of ignorance, and a soul of impurity – an incomplete Being bound within the walls of limitation, or do we see an entity who is God-governed and God-made, who is the medium of Light, the instrument of Love, the ideal of Divine Creation placed forever on the plains of illimitability?

And once we've generated this image, how long can we maintain it – a few fleeting moments in a day, once or twice a week, all the time? Indeed, to discipline our minds so that we see only the Divine and Infinite, not the mortal and finite, is a great challenge. Yet, such an image will uplift us, lighten our hearts, increase our vibration and, unequivocally, enhance the quality of life.

Richard Andrew King

THE GLASS LENS

"Father, I hate that man. Can I strike him down?"

"Why, my son? What has he done to you?"

"Nothing to me, but his discourtesy, jealousy, hate, create a passion in my mind which cannot find peace."

"My son, all men are as a pane of glass, cut perfectly shaped and sized; clear, transparent in their Maker's hands, reflectors for their Maker's eyes."

"Why then, my Father, do I see such inequity?"

"Because, my son, you only see the soil upon the lens. What would your eyes behold if the glass were cleansed?"

"If there were no dirt to cover up the light, undoubtedly I could only see perfection in my sight."

"And when you hate a man, my son, do you hate him for his sins? Rather, you should love the man and see no dirt upon the lens."

"What then, my Father, should I do for the Brotherhood of Men?"

The Karate Consciousness

"Simply cleanse the lens and see perfection, for it only is in the cleaning of the glass that you'll find peace at last."

When the student controls his mental faculties to maintain this image, he will know what Divinity is. He will touch the garment of Perfection.

Mental discipline is obviously not restricted to our perception of others. Anything we think is subject to regulation. In fact, our entire thought spectrum should be intensely self-scrutinized. For quality living, our minds should be saturated with love, life, peace, joy, harmony, strength, health, abundance, freedom, non-limitation. As these concepts are held in our minds, they will eventually appear as experience in our existence. This is the law – we are what we think.

The discipline and control needed to place these thoughts wholly within our minds varies, of course, with each person. But the moment at hand is not too soon for anyone to initiate the exercise. It is a matter of individual choice, but this experience we call living will never get any better until we assume command of our minds, discipline our mental faculties, and so control our thoughts that there is absolutely no avenue open for anything except the ethereal and supernal.

Student of life, monitor your thoughts! Excise concepts and ideals contrary to your divinity. Close the door to the ebony veils of

Richard Andrew King

darkness and open wide the door to Light. This you must do by yourself and for yourself because, in the final analysis, you are the master of your fate; you are the captain of your soul.

THE GLOWING FEELING

The discipline of the mind is important. However, the mind, as instrument of the intellect, is only a part of the life system. The heart – center of compassion, feeling and love – must not be abandoned. Balance is a major principle in assuring the Flow, and neither mind nor heart should create an imbalance.

It is just as important to feel as it is to think. Yet, the art of feeling often is subordinated to intellect. There are many problems, however, which cannot be solved purely by intellect. A warm smile, a light touch, a pat on the back, the shedding and sharing of a tear are, oftentimes, the only solutions to some problems.

Man, especially in a technocracy as we have today where importance is placed on mental faculties and sterile technologies, would do well to discipline his consciousness in order to achieve a balance between thought and feeling. To love, to feel, to show compassion is as necessary to a well-functioning life system as the ingestion of nutrients or the process of thought. Let us, therefore, feel as well as think and apply the concept of discipline and control to each.

TARGET CENTER

Perhaps one of the best descriptions of a Master is a person who can hit the center of the target, whatever it may be, every time and accomplish what he sets out to do. Through the D.C. Factor and the principle of "focus" he can succeed. To focus on anything is to locate the center point and direct all attention and energy to it.

This principle of focus in application is beautiful. It can be utilized correctly to achieve maximum efficiency in any problem-solving situation. The karateka uses this principle whenever he delivers a blow. Through the application of focus he can achieve varied degrees of power, as well as a myriad of effects.

To hit *target center* there must be the proper aim and concentration. The secret, if it can be called that, is the position of the focal point. It is this fact that separates an expert from a novice and allows for the successful solution of any problem, all else being equal.

For example, in delivering a strike to any target, if the focal point of the strike, kick, punch, chop, etc., is in front of or at the point of contact, the impact on the target would be light to nil. If, however, the focal point is not "to" the target but "through" it, the damage would be considerable. *Not to but through* is an excellent Kiado-Ryu adage for generating maximum power to a target.

Richard Andrew King

The same holds true for problem-solving in daily life. If we focus "through" the problem, not just to it, the odds of success are highly possible. We must go beyond the point of contact to be successful. Think of sprinters. They run *through* the finish line; not *to* the finish line. The same is true for solving any problem. We must go *through it*, not just to it.

How can this principle of *focus* be transferred to daily problems? Simply by visualizing, conceiving or perceiving the problem as solved and completed. Individual energy, then, at the outset of the solution, is aimed at the manifested solution, not the problem. If the problem is concentrated upon, there will never be or can never be a solution because all energy will be focused on the problem rather than on the solution. Therefore, think solution! Discipline and control the mind so all force is directed *through* the problem to a focal point of solution. By these means the student of life will hit target center every time and move closer to the title of Master.

THE FRONTIER

The greatest of all frontiers is Divine Perfection. The reaching of this frontier will not occur by luck or good fortune but by desire and the continue search for and manifestation of higher truths and ideals.

Along the road to this goal, each student is required to learn total self-discipline and control. However, he must not allow himself to be trapped within the walls of limitation and contemporary mass hypnotism whatever the age or era.

In today's society man is challenged to learn many things on the road to self-mastery and move from the world of the warrior to the manifestation of the Mystic Master. In this regard, the D.C. Factor will play a vital role in the process.

Richard Andrew King

The Karate Consciousness

Chapter 9

STRENGTH

S trength is internal power manifested in external form. As all qualities of Divine Individuality, it flows from the center of man's Oneness with his Creator. It permeates all components of the life system – physical, mental, spiritual – and is the sustaining force in the quest for perfection.

It is an absolute necessity for the student to continually increase his strength if he is to successfully progress in the continuum. New obstacles and challenges on the vertical growth pattern always yield an increased functional understanding of the life force once they are surpassed, but to conquer them demands a degree of strength equal to each task. Therefore, the goal for each individual

Richard Andrew King

aspiring to mastery is to continually seek to increase the flow from the Source because, of itself, the Source is strength and man is only as strong as his ability to align himself with it.

SHEDDING THE OLD SKIN

As each new age dawns upon man, new concepts are acquired. The process of this acquisition is not always easy because the old, which was at one time the new, must be discarded for the momentary new.

The kind of strength needed in today's world is different from that which was needed in past times. Animal strength and its manifestations are no longer in vogue. Simply, they are becoming outdated because mankind is acquiring the garments of a higher form of strength.

The old concept of strength was expressed in physically strong and rugged characteristics, in the ability never to weep or exhibit tender feeling emotion, and in the capability to emerge victorious at all cost, even at the sacrifice of integrity, intellect and enlightenment. This may have helped man conquer geographical, primitive, earth-bound frontiers but it will not be of any help in conquering the frontier of self-mastery.

The mortal human ego, based on the old concept of strength, has always been the epitome of fragility. When humans have appeared strong, it has not been their humanness which generated the strength but divine essence penetrating the veil of their mortality. When man sheds the rags of his mortality and clothes himself in the garments of immortality – love, life and light – he will truly be strong because strength is a natural characteristic of the immortal and the divine.

The higher ideal of strength finds itself not centered in animal prowess but gentleness. This is true strength because it takes more internal power, discipline and control to be gentle than it does to be hard, coarse, caustic, abusive, etc. The gentle spirit is the one which has recognized the need for refinement in the nature of man. Gentleness is love acting. This is not to say that there are not times when a more rigid and austere posture is necessary but, generally speaking, there is too much of the latter and not enough of the former. As the student strives to effect gentleness, he will see how difficult it is to develop and maintain, but he will also see how beautiful life can be when gentleness is the established norm. Strive to be gentle! This is the epitome of true power and the noble characteristic of the glorified soul.

Gentleness may be defined as love and moderation. Love is the great vibration; moderation, the key to balance. Having already discussed these two principles of life, it is easy to understand why gentleness is a meaningful definition of strength. Therefore, if strength is gentleness, and gentleness is love and moderation, it follows that strength is love and moderation. Thus, it is easy to see why a Master is strong – he is the epitome of love and moderation.

Richard Andrew King

Contrary to this idea is the concept that he who is strong is domineering, i.e., overbearing and arrogant. But the domineering individual is not strong. Contrarily, he is the antithesis of strength. Ostensibly, he is powerful because he seems to dominate others, but in reality he is only attempting to find strength by exhibiting power in the flock. The genuinely strong individual doesn't need to be domineering. He has found his power within the center of his divine Being, not without.

Let it be understood that gentleness is not being flimsy and weak. Nor is it an avoidance of power. It is the control of power – that dynamic universal force which perpetuates life and flows unceasingly into form. Again, gentleness is not the abuse, misuse or avoidance of power. It is the control and divinely creative use of it.

The gentle person is highly disciplined. He has learned to transmute and channel energy in ways which promote the quality of life, not destroy, defame or deprecate it. He is truly enlightened and an invaluable asset to society. He is to be appreciated, applauded and exemplified, for he is the ideal of the new-age man.

THE ABILITIES

To gain a further understanding of strength, a catalogue of some of its skills may be helpful. Strength is the ability to endure and persevere; to be flexible; to be firm; to feel; to surrender the outer and claim the inner; to admit wrongdoing or injustice when self-generated and apologize for it; to remain steadfast to personal convictions; to stand alone; to stand amid the crowd; to love and be loved; to allow others to be themselves; to take one more step – to carry on when dawn cannot be seen; to discipline the self; to speak the truth; to do what is right; to be patient; to be resilient, i.e., to bounce back after failure and defeat; to stand within the tumultuous cry of mortality and proclaim the right to life, love and light.

Tomorrow is not soon enough to begin the development of strength in body, mind or spirit. It is axiomatic that tomorrow never comes. All action occurs within the forever Here and Now. Therefore, to put off in the future what can be done in the moment is antithetical to progress. Immediate action is the only solution to procrastination.

Physical strength is the easiest to develop because we can see, feel and touch the body, which is a rather concrete idea of mortality and the human spectrum, whereas the mind (intellect) and spirit are more abstract and, therefore, pose a greater challenge to the development of strength. Exercise and participation in athletics on a regular basis, whether organized or unorganized, will enhance bodily strength.

The mind may be strengthened by thinking. To catalyze the thought process, questions beginning with the words why, what,

Richard Andrew King

how and so forth are quite effectual. The key is not simply asking the question but in seeking the answer.

For instance, it's easy to ask, "Who am I?" but it's not so easy for most of us to give an intelligent answer beyond stating our names. Other questions may be, "Why am I?" "Why do people really die?" "How can immortality be achieved?" "What is intelligence?" "What is God?" Certainly, in answering these questions the mind must grow. It would be impossible for it not to.

Spirit is to the mass consciousness the most abstract of the three components of the life system. However, as one's individual Being gradually departs the planes of mortality and moves upward into the planes of immortality, spirit will appear less abstract until it is eventually perceived as concrete reality.

The essence of Spirit is God – the all-pervading power, intelligence and substance of the universe. To develop a strength of spirit is more demanding than mere physical or mental exercise. To hold God in consciousness, to cogitate and meditate on God is important. However, we must also learn to act, to instantaneously respond to His dictates. We must align ourselves with our Creator, and in the Oneness we will achieve the highest degree of strength possible.

If the student believes he is created in the image and likeness of God, then he must also understand he is of the same substance. Therefore, to be strong he must simply let the Power flow; he must

The Karate Consciousness

invigorate and fortify the presence of God in his life. He does this in part by going within and continually making greater contact with the Source which originates from within, from the center of his Being.

FOCAL POINTS

All power flows from the center of Being. If this truth were more readily acknowledged, the mass consciousness would exhibit greater strength. Yet, the focal point of the amalgamated contemporary mind is focused on externalities, on what is located without, not within.

Man today seeks comforts for his body and its array of sensations rather than comforts for this soul. He chases illusions or temporal realities when, for his own well-being, he should be concentrating upon the reality of internal infinite existence.

A simple illustration of this is the individual who dresses in beautiful exquisite garments but allows his/her body to atrophy, to become weak and frail. Additionally, there is the person who, for the sake of excitement and a release of energy, goes everywhere and does everything, vainly trying to pervade the entire spectrum of mortal existence to find thrills and exhilarations. Little is it known that the most intense exhilarations of life, the most sensational experiences, reside in that place which is no farther than the center of individual Being. We cannot grow on the

Richard Andrew King

vertical tangent or increase our vibration if we continually avoid the Center. The passageway to infinity lies within. Therefore, in relation to divine progress the admonition is, "Bring it on Home!"

It is through prayer, meditation and thoughtful contemplation that we assist ourselves in reaching the supreme focal point of Being, i.e., God. But to pray, meditate and think requires discipline, control and the power to release ourselves from the pull of external forces. This we develop a little at a time but each little step eventually results in a monumental stride. Therefore, we must continue to persevere, to unceasingly take one less step in the realm of temporal external illusion substituted by one more step into the territory of internal reality and power. As we proceed along this path, we shall consequently emerge strong and unmistakenly powerful.

Extended strength is stamina, endurance. It is a characteristic we all need because the journey though the continuum is not a sprint. It is a marathon. One, single, solitary exhibition of strength may result in the conquest of one, maybe two, obstacles, but it will not suffice for the long run. We need staying power, not for five years, ten, twenty, forty or even a hundred years but forever. Strange? Not really when one lives totally within the concept of infinity.

We can generate stamina by focusing our minds on perpetuity and inexhaustibility. In other words, we must visualize our strength as never departing from us but remaining a constant characteristic of our nature. To think of our strength as limited or finite will preclude us from great deeds, for always the greatest tasks demand the greatest strength.

It is probably a valid generalization that most individuals don't realize how strong they actually are. Primarily, this is because they've never been tested to their limits. The experienced karateka should be able to testify to this statement because only as he advances in the study of the art does he learn how to draw power from within himself to generate considerable force. He doesn't have to create it because it already exists naturally in limitless quantities. He just must learn how to give it an avenue of meaningful expression.

We are all intrinsically strong. The only difference in those who demonstrate high levels of strength is that they have learned how to tap the Source. They've learned that if an individual pushes himself to his furthest limit he will surpass his limitations, thus annihilating any concept of limitation in his experience. And as he continues to overcome more distant and difficult obstacles, he becomes proportionally stronger.

Therefore, the admonition is for the student to challenge himself and push back the barriers of his current understanding and to keep pushing them back eternally. This is the path to the development of strength.

Richard Andrew King

THE NON-PROOF POSE

The bearer of strength does not have to prove himself to the world or to anyone in it. He traverses the road of life with a calm, firm posture and fortified resolve.

Oftentimes, however, it is quite noticeable that in the realm of flock power individuals feel it is important to prove their strength to others, if not to themselves. Karate, because it is a vehicle for the development of internal power, is attractive to people so disposed. They study the art only to assist in the expansion of their own egos. This is, indeed, unfortunate, and the sincere student should realize this propensity. In fact, one of the purposes of karate is to help the student grow out of this predicament so he can truly appreciate life. If he is truly sincere, he cannot help but realize that as he learns more of the art and more of this internal power he has absolutely no need to prove his power to anyone or anything. Of himself he is powerful. He knows this and lives, therefore, within the concept of the "Non-Proof Pose."

NEW AGE HERO

A hero, traditionally, has always been epitomized by his strength. Weak heroes have never existed. The heroes of the new age, be they male or female, will, likewise, be characterized by their strength. However, the brawny, physically rugged Herculean type hero will not be in vogue. Times have changed. Animal prowess is rapidly giving way to the higher ideals of gentleness, love, compassion, justice, enlightenment. The idea of the hero has eclipsed the physical realm and is moving upward into the more ethereal planes of consciousness. Look for him or her. Perhaps he may be found across the street or around the corner but, then again, the unmistakable form of the new-age hero may well be found within the reflected personal image of the mirror on the wall.

Richard Andrew King

The Karate Consciousness

Chapter 10

PRIORITIES

&

POSSESSIONS

The quest for, and establishment of, Divine Perfection within individual Being is a challenge demanding the correct alignment of priorities and the proper perspective of personal possessions. An enlightened consciousness and the functional demonstrability of the life force pertaining to it cannot be acquired by chance or monetary consideration. Enlightenment is a matter of personal development and learning.

Richard Andrew King

The game of immortality is a totally different contest from the game of mortality. The rules are different. The methodology is different. The rewards are different. Such a challenge demands of the student a shift in focus and living habits from those to which he may be accustomed. This is not to say that he should drop everything he's doing and embark on a totally different path recklessly indifferent to consequences. Prudence does warrant practicality. But it does mean to suggest, in this particular case, that the student reevaluate his priorities and his propensity to material possessions and subordinate them to those things which result in an increased, edified, enlightened consciousness and the generation of a concomitant vibration. It does not necessarily mean he should give anything up or away – simply realign his energies and mental focus to coincide with more ethereal concepts and ideals until he receives definite revelations as to his own well-being, growth and divine blueprint.

The unnecessary complexity of today's society seems to strengthen the structure of already misaligned priorities. People are constantly getting, spending and dispersing their energies in such a myriad of mortal directions that the universal life forces flowing through them cannot coalesce into one main stream. This is, indeed, unfortunate, especially for those people who are caught up in the momentum. But, nonetheless, it is a current reality which must be faced head on, not with the hope that conditions improve but with the firm resolution to make them improve.

Karate offers viable assistance in this regard. The discipline and control it teaches can be utilized to help the individual break away and remain separate from life styles and thought patterns which are not conducive to healthy living. Too, it does offer an incipient, functional understanding of what mastery is all about so the student of life may continue to progress in his own self-development after he has left the confines of the karate milieu.

At any time, however, in his study of karate and/or life, the sentient student will begin to inquire as to the feasibility of establishing anything but priorities based on illimitability and infinity when he exists in an infinite universe. In other words, it doesn't make sense to have priorities which are finite in scope when the universe is infinite. Such a relationship is incongruous. An infinite universe demands priorities which are infinite.

THE PRIORTIES

What, then, are the priorities which should be entertained in an infinite universe? From the author's viewpoint there is only one around which all others are formed. This initial priority, this matter which must take precedence over all others, is for each individual to possess an ever-expanding consciousness of God – Love, Life and Light – and to continually strive to become a greater transparency for the passage of Divine radiance. At its core, life is energy. We are energy. The Power that created everything is energy, i.e., God is energy. The ultimate goal of life is to merge into that omniscient, omnipotent, omnipresent universal energy that created us. There is no higher goal than such a Divine Merging.

To maintain such a priority is to focus on all that is good, just, equitable, true and eternal. A consciousness so tuned will always grow on the vertical tangent. It is impossible for it to do otherwise.

As each individual is centered in continually expanding the expression of love, life and light, the quality of his experience in the continuum must, likewise, expand. Therefore, the future will hold only hope, optimism and the reality of greater living. To hold an ever-increasing consciousness of God, immortality, divinity and eternality is a rich blessing, and the greatest of all possessions in the forever Here and Now.

Could there be a greater possession than this? Certainly it would be magnificent to express Divine Oneness to its fullest, and all shall who aspire to radiate the Light, but what levels of attainment are there beyond this worldly level? Certainly, personal growth and a functional demonstrability of the life force does not stop with material attainment. Therefore, to always be in possession of an expanding God energy must be the most grand gift, indeed.

The karateka who is sincerely dedicated to personal development will one day arrive at this conclusion. With such a realization his hands will have given wings to his mind and he can then pursue the course of ethereal flight.

The Karate Consciousness

As a continual God consciousness is maintained as the first priority, the karateka will obviously have to subordinate the desire for worldly accoutrements, awards, designations and titles to a higher goal; not denounce or eliminate them, simply subordinate them to a more elevated purpose.

Even if legitimately attained, all worldly trappings are still symbols of earthly recognition. To be acknowledged by outside sources has its place, but more important is the degree of self-realization and enlightenment the student has achieved.

Ultimately, the individual should not lose perspective. If he is always looking for external forces, organizations or entities to praise him, judge him, or pour accolades upon him, he is separating himself from the concept of self-integration and wholeness, which is basic to his expression of Divine Perfection. God first and foremost; everything else behind. This is the rule.

Moreover, to be God-conscious totally decimates any need for material idols, symbols or human applause. This may seem theoretical but anyone who has ever been so centered will testify as to its validity. In fact, when the student is so disposed, idols and symbols are meaningless. The only real thing of value is to express Love, radiate Light and manifest Life in increasing proportions. It's like being offered an automobile when you can travel at thought-speed flight. Who needs it?

Richard Andrew King

So the admonition here is relatively obvious: the student should strive to be less concerned with what is gained and shown outwardly and primarily concerned with what is attained inwardly and which creates, sustains and beautifies existence. An ever-expanding consciousness of God – this is the first priority.

The placement of individual focus in such a manner has a major and, perhaps, unforeseen benefit. The knowledge, wisdom and understanding gained by such a divine focal point quite often alleviates many problems and perturbations occurring at lower levels.

For example, by generating a vibration of love, all hate and its concomitant expressions vanish. They do not have to be wrestled with, worried about or entertained. They simply disappear, just as darkness does when beset with light.

For instance, in likeness to the former analogy, by possessing telepathic abilities the problem of finding a phone or other communication device to connect with another person evaporates. Advanced spiritual technology, or to coin a new word, *Divinology*, obviates lesser skills. Thus, in seeking the higher laws and principles of life, we remove ourselves from problems associated with lower life levels without having to solve the problem per se. In other words, the natural process of ascension will resolve many problems and predicaments which could not be solved otherwise.

The Karate Consciousness

The second aspect of the first priority is for the individual to continually strive to become a greater transparency for the passage of Divine radiance. To the skeptic or agnostic the phrase "Divine Radiance" may simply be regarded as a poetic euphemism relating to some obscure or unknown theory. This may be relatively true, for at the vibratory level of normal human life Divine Radiance is rather obscure and unknown. But as the individual elevates himself to higher states of consciousness, it will become a definite and known reality.

For all of those Beings who dwell in the deepest and darkest niche of the cave, and have for ages, it is often difficult to convince them there is such a thing as light. Reality for them is darkness, and it always will be until they escape the ebony veil of the cave. But the light does exist and no amount of obstinate denial or ignorance will alter this truth.

Divine Radiance is just that, radiance – lustrous, brilliant, white light, earth-shattering in its magnitude and power; incomparable to any light source known to the material consciousness. It is real and its essence will excite much investigation by anyone who has experienced it. The key, it would seem, is for each student of life to become as pure a transparency as possible for it because, as it passes through one's individual Being, it increases vibration and, correspondingly, lifts the individual to higher levels of consciousness and bequeaths to him an understanding of reality beyond the human condition.

Richard Andrew King

To possess an ever-expanding consciousness of God is to also be centered in the realms of peace, purity, virtue, strength, courage, harmony, balance, integrity, truth, understanding, sincerity, humility, kindness, compassion, gentleness, abundance, power, divine authority, health and freedom. The all inclusive term for these attributes is "holiness," the state of being divinely whole, complete and functionally integrated as a living Being.

It is these things which are man's true possessions. They are, indeed, treasures which cannot be stolen. Ironically and justifiably, however, neither can they be purchased, and all who would acquire them must travel the same basic road.

Where there is a divinely rich person these attributes will exist. There will also be another distinctive quality – the ability to see beauty in all things and to exhibit it. In architecture, dance, music, literature, attitude, inter-personal relationships, vibration – wherever God is, there is beauty. Rely on the divinely wealthy person to acknowledge it, accentuate it and give it form.

As the student rises in his consciousness, he will acquire this desire to create beauty and with its creation will acquire a warm sense of excitement and joy. Such a feeling cannot come with the creation of discord, hatred, fear, dishonesty and so forth because these things are not natural to the God-centered person. However, when beauty is generated it's like coming home after years of an extended absence. In fact, it is coming home to Spirit – the source of all creation. This is the reason for the joy and a feeling of genuine accomplishment. It is in this return to Source that one realizes his true heritage and that the possession of an ever-expanding consciousness of God is the greatest of all priorities – always beautiful, meaningful, joyful; never futile.

THE FUTILITY TUNNELS

The continuum is filled with many avenues, all of which are forever open to the interested mind. They cannot be closed because man does have free will – the ability to choose for himself, by himself, the roads he wishes to traverse. However, all of these avenues do not return to the Source. Many are, in themselves, traps and snares. Others parallel the abyss of oblivion. Some of these are not roads of infinite life landscaped in beauty, peace, joy and love. They are, more explicitly, Tunnels of Futility embellished in frustration, anxiety, disease, hatred, discord, emptiness, pain and death. Ostensibly, they are paths of promise. Their mortal magnetism and wide-open doors receive all incomers with hospitality, but the beverages served therein are saturated with poisons and drugs which blind, deafen and desensitize the wayfarer in an attempt to detain him from finding the true way home.

The emanations from these tunnels reek in arrogance, pride, envy, ignorance, injustice, darkness. Needless to say, these avenues are deleterious to individual well-being. They all have dead ends, and once they've been traversed at some length it is doubly difficult to find the way back. Even the Greek Thesean technique of attaching a string to the mouth of a cave in order to find one's way out of the cave by following the string back to its initial attachment may prove inadequate. Strings break and are easily severed. In all, it is a labyrinthine experience of confusion, despondency and despair and one which should be avoided.

The one major characteristic of these futility tunnels is that they are all centered in the realm of external appearance and experience. Money, power in the flock, prestige, titles, positions, material possessions and mortal pleasures are all things which often become the driving forces in people's lives.

There are also other similarities between them. Firstly, none of them can be taken with the individual as he makes his ascension to higher levels, or lower levels for that matter. They must be left behind when the human body dies. What a waste it is to spend part or all of an entire life primarily devoted to their expression and acquisition when the time devoted to them could be used more efficiently in the promotion and development of divinity.

Individuals have amassed fortunes in money, real estate, jewels, material goods, corporate enterprises, etc., only to have their belongings and holdings vanish when they pass on. The Biblical saying rings true, *What does it profit a man if he gains the whole world but loses his own soul?* (KJV-Bible: St. Matthew 16:26)

The Karate Consciousness

Secondly, all of these futility tunnels are finite in dimension. They are neither infinite nor eternal. Hence, to concentrate on them is to preclude personal development. Being finite, they are in contradiction to the spirit, which is limitless. It is, therefore, unnatural for anyone to focus on them.

Thirdly, they only allow people to expand on the horizontal growth plane. A person may pursue such lateral expansion to great lengths, but as long as he keeps developing along this line he will not be able to advance vertically. This horizontal tangent is typified by the mortal spectrum. In all of his years of earthly existence a person may become worldly-wise but this is all he will become. He will know nothing about the divinity or levels of existence far superior to this one.

Knowledge of mundane things is also quite temporal. One ounce of divine understanding will eclipse and falsify a thousand years of global intellect. It really is nonsensical to expend so much valuable energy on such a fleeting concern as worldly priorities.

Fourthly, none of these subjects of study will increase individual vibration or ethereal consciousness. In fact, they work to contrary ends. Individuals mesmerized by power in the flock, for instance, dissipate the very energy they need in order to increase their vibration rate. Consumed by a desire to control others or enhance their own egos, they fail to bring all of their energy, intellect and resources to focus on expanding their own inner awareness. Energy passing through them is thus diverted from the internal path, where it should be, to the external one where it will only dissipate or find expression in temporal things.

Lacking in vibration, the consciousness cannot rise to higher levels of functionability. Thus, it will remain trapped where it is on the mortal planes of existence subject to all of the manifestations generated at that level. Growth will remain stagnate, and the possibility of a life of peace, joy, harmony, abundance, freedom, holiness and so forth will continue to be a matter of conjecture, speculation and intellectual philosophizing.

Fifthly, those who continue to wander further into the Tunnels of Futility will find themselves drifting into an increasingly hollow existence. The farther they recede from the light the more empty they become because man is Spirit, Love, Life and Light. To experience fullness and joy he must remain in them. To separate himself from them only creates misery, frustration and despondency. To be continually happy, man must remain at the Source. It's unfortunate but sometimes he doesn't realize this until he is standing on a precipice overlooking the abyss of oblivion. The road back is often perilous but it is a journey he knows he must make at all cost. There can be no rest until man has returned to a state of Oneness with his Creator.

In avoiding the Tunnels of Futility the student should remember that it's not what he has that counts in the way of material riches, power, prestige, position, but what he is and what he has attained in the pursuit of his divinity. Much of the mass consciousness of

The Karate Consciousness

today is mesmerized and stumbles in the ebony veil of the labyrinth. Like the deepest cave dwellers, such souls feel that what they possess is reality and their beliefs are the final word about existence. So be it. They are their own judge, jury and executioner. But their mistakes must be avoided and the process of avoidance is found in establishing an ever-expanding consciousness of God as the first priority of living.

THE CHANGING OF THE TIDE

Procrastination in the realignment of priorities is detrimental to the success of the project. Traveling down the Tunnels of Futility only enhances the momentum and carries the individual farther away from the Source. The desire to stop and reverse the energy flow may become extremely difficult, especially when the experiences on the road back may appear quite daunting. The flow, however, must be reversed, and there is never any time like the present. In fact, the present is the only valid tense of time.

When the commitment is made to reverse the momentum by restructuring individual priorities, progress may seem slow at first. This is quite natural. It's like running down a hill at full speed, bringing yourself to a complete stop, turning around and running back up the hill. The stress generated in the process of stopping can be quite severe and, of course, when "putting on the brakes" there is still no progress in the reverse direction.

Richard Andrew King

However, as the brakes are applied, the momentum of futility does decrease which, in itself, is a success. Too, while turning around to begin running in the opposite direction there is, as yet, no momentum created in the positive direction but, still, the preparation for resuming the race is accomplished, which is necessary.

Finally, after coming to a halt and turning around, the process of rechanneling energy to generate momentum in the right direction can begin. Now things start to pick up. The moral of the analogy: don't become discouraged and don't expect results too soon. Besides, after all that running there will probably be a time needed for rest and revitalization. During this period, patience is seen for the virtue it is. Bear in mind that the restructuring of priorities and the regeneration of momentum along the path of Love, Life and Light takes time. However, it is a meaningful process and one which is quite unavoidable for the divine aspirant.

THE SUBSTITUTION-DISSOLUTION PRINCIPLE

The process of realigning priorities can be thoroughly challenging. One principle which may be helpful is *Substitution-Dissolution*.

To attempt to suppress a desire associated with the futility tunnels may, in itself, prove futile. Desires cannot really be successfully suppressed because the energy which fuels the desire needs to have an avenue of expression. We all know what happens when

The Karate Consciousness

we cannot vent our emotions in positive ways. We often implode or explode but in either case the result can be damaging. Therefore, to attempt to suppress a desire for material riches, for instance, may have extensive and unwholesome repercussions within the individual life system. The correct procedure for handling such a condition would be to substitute an avenue through which the energy can pass and, thus, find expression. The old desire will naturally dissolve with the passage of time.

For instance, by focusing on love or life development rather than the accumulation of riches, the energy which fueled and sustained the latter now ignites the former. The energy has an outlet. A momentum of love and life is generated while the momentum for riches withers and gradually dies like the embers of an unattended campfire. In this way the process of realignment is made easier and the probability of discomfort lessened.

THE GUIDING RULE

If there is ever any confusion as to the establishment of personal priorities, the student will do well to remember this Guiding Rule: *Focus only on those qualities which will remain with you as you journey through the continuum rising from level to level; avoid placing any exaggerated emphasis on things which, by their very nature, must be left behind.* This is the most expedient method of ascent.

Richard Andrew King

In analysis, those things which must be left behind are mortal egos, pride, sensuality, earthly titles, political positions, dollar bills and automobiles. Those which may be taken with you on the infinite journey are the things of Spirit: love, life, light, peace, purity, harmony, discipline, control, courage, humility, strength, virtue, a willingness to learn and grow, a sense of freedom and liberty, a desire to serve, and a mind focused on perfection. These are the priorities and possessions, the gifts of an infinite, universal Creator bestowed on its children.

Chapter 11

TEACHING

The teaching of karate is, unequivocally, a responsibility. Because of its potentially violent nature, it is a subject which must be handled delicately to keep things in perspective, especially with young people. Teaching, therefore, demands professionalization and professionalism, thoughtful contemplation, and a dedication to the concepts of higher consciousness, individuality, freedom, perfection, excellence, student well-being and enhancement.

Like karate, teaching in itself is an art. To be a practitioner of karate is one thing; to be a teacher of it is quite another, indeed, and those who teach or desire to teach should be aware of this

Richard Andrew King

distinction. They owe it not just to themselves but to their students and, therefore, every sincere karate instructor should consider addressing himself to three major areas: 1. subject matter; 2. professionalization; 3. student emphasis.

SUBJECT KNOWLEDGE

The instructor of karate, as any professional, must know his art. This does not mean he must be a champion competitor. Many great craftsmen and champions in every field of endeavor do not have the ability to teach, although they are, indeed, the exemplum of their chosen art.

However, it does mean the teacher should have a sound and thorough working understanding of the subject matter he is teaching. He should also possess the understanding of how this knowledge can be transferred to everyday practical experiences if it can be.

For example, the karateka in a teaching role should be aware of discipline, control, concentration, focus, coordination, humility, flexibility, relaxability, reactability, adaptability, strength, endurance, perseverance, integrity, flow, balance, harmony, peace, love, and how to transfer these to the exigencies of living if he is to be an effective instructor. It is not enough just to give a person a little knowledge. The real key is in showing him how to utilize such knowledge to achieve greater levels of expression of the life force.

The knowledge barrier in karate, as in most every field, is nonexistent. There is a great myriad of styles of martial arts, ranging from what are generally regarded as the "hard" styles of Japan, Okinawa and Korea, to the "soft" styles of kung fu in China, to the "medium" styles of kenpo and its variations, to the redirectional style of aikido, to the pugilistic environment of boxing, to the world of mixed martial arts, to name a few. The landscape of martial arts covers a wide spectrum of interests, styles and techniques, and there is a style for just about any temperament, ability and disposition.

However, it is not the style which is the important aspect of teaching. Style should only be considered as a vehicle to learning about life and the aforementioned principles and concepts. In the past, much ado has been made about which style is superior or better than all of the others. But this is only a manifestation of the Power in the Flock Syndrome. Individual learning, growth and edification are the focal points of all serious and enlightened teaching, not style.

Subject knowledge is also variable and timely depending upon which level of learning the student is on. What is applicable to a three-year student is generally not suitable for a beginner and vice-versa. The experienced karateka must, of course, never lose sight of basics, just as any artisan or professional would not, but his level of learning obviously surpasses that of the novice.

It is good for the new student and the teacher to understand this concept of *suitable knowledge*. Oftentimes, a beginning student will want to learn what he sees experienced karatekas doing. But to do so may jeopardize his well-being and development. First things must come first, and things which often look easy are, oftentimes, the result of years, if not decades, of training, development and experience. Enter Patience; exit Hurry.

The concept of a Black Belt also deserves some attention here. This symbol of achievement has been so blown out of proportion that the higher ideal of learning as a priority has had little opportunity to take hold in the contemporary karate consciousness. The amount and type of knowledge and degree of expertise required to attain a Black Belt varies considerably from system to system, school to school, instructor to instructor. Thus, it loses its significance and, as far as a valuable measurement of capability and attainment is concerned, it approaches obscurity.

The Black Belt has also become a status symbol, unfortunately for the wrong reason. To many people it is the epitome of physical prowess and deadly skill, when it should be a symbol acknowledging attainment of the art's knowledge and demonstrability as well as humility, internal power and a relatively increased understanding of the life force.

The Karate Consciousness

The attainment of a Black Belt is not the end of a student's learning, quite to the contrary. It is the beginning because its achievement implies that the student has progressed in his understanding to the point of discarding physical prowess and power in the flock as creative tools for the life force and acquired the functional understanding of surrender to divine, creative principles and their ensuing manifestations and expressions.

However, the contemporary consciousness believes it is an end, oftentimes in itself. This is incorrect, and the student of karate should realize from the start of his training that his education in the art and his acquisition of a Black Belt – if such a symbol is used in his system – is only a beginning to the infinite journey of personal unfoldment and development. It is only a symbol of recognition, not a crown of mortal glorification. The crown (of light) comes with Divinity, not mortality.

Regarding this aspect of the subject matter of karate, there is a warning: students and teachers should be careful of treading too deeply and too long into the mortal aspects of the art, i.e., bodily harm, injury, death blows and so forth. Spending three thousand years studying mortality and lethality will not necessarily help someone strive toward and achieve meaningful rewards on the immortality spectrum. The purpose of life is to move up in vibration and consciousness, not down, and thereby achieve greater expression of Divine principles and Being. Concentration on subject matter which is antithetical to this end will obviously

Richard Andrew King

preclude its possibility. Not destruction but construction is the aim.

Too, it should be remembered that when the student feels it is time to move on to other experiences affording opportunities for growth, he must leave karate behind. The cord is to be severed eventually because if it is not, the individual cannot be free to ascend to higher levels. The art of karate is simply a vehicle whose purpose is transportation along the path of personal development.

A final note to both student and teacher is that knowledge is a temporal thing. Unlike love, it is subject to change and decay. It is relative for different levels and plateaus of existence. Be discerning of its impact, cautious as to its reality, and wise in its use.

PROFESSIONALISM

Perhaps if there is anything lacking in the teaching of karate, it is professionalization. There are karate professionals but few professional teachers of the art.

A teacher in a professional sense is an individual who has had adequate training and education and, correspondingly, an equivalent amount of expertise in the realm of teaching. This demands that he be schooled in educational psychology, theories of learning, methodology, socio-economic variables, measurement

The Karate Consciousness

and evaluation and so forth. It is inconceivable that an individual can teach well if he has no functional understanding of the learning process. Preferably, he should possess corroborating evidence as to his authenticity as a teacher.

This does not mean he must have a college or university degree, advanced degrees or teaching credentials, but such evidence does testify to a certain amount of expertise. There are teachers who are "natural" or "born" teachers. They know instinctively how to teach and their expertise is directly visible in their pupils, but they are rare.

Even so, the "born" teacher will always seek to better his ability. In our society this is generally done through some form of higher education at the college level. At any rate, such accouterments are a plus factor and any individual seeking to study the art of karate or parents sending their children to a martial arts school would be wise to investigate any instructor to ascertain his or her credentials and qualifications.

Any teacher will be much better able to instruct his students if he has an understanding of the learning process. How does the pupil learn? This is an ineluctable question for the teacher, and the answer should lead to educational efficiency, the result of which will be student progress, learning and personal development.

Richard Andrew King

There are many learning theories. Three basic ones are the following: 1. stimulus-response; 2. response-stimulus; 3. gestalt field.

The first is usually labeled S-R. In this theory a need or drive (the stimulus) seeks a reduction (the response). For example, a person having a need or drive to defend himself against physical aggression may seek karate as the means to reduce the need. As he or she becomes skilled in physical defense, the need to defend oneself decreases. In a different perspective an instructor may have a need to see his students excel. His need is the stimulus; the achievement of excellence on the part of his students is the response and, likewise, the reward.

The response-stimulus theory, often referred to as operant conditioning, is just the reverse. The individual is stimulated, rewarded, when he gives the proper response. For example, if a karateka is studying for a green belt (the stimulus) he will not achieve it until he issues the correct response which, in this case, would be a variety of responses depending upon the system of karate he is studying.

The same principle is true in the field of politics in a democracy. As an aspiring politician conveys the image or supports policies the people desire (the response), the people, in turn, elect the official, their vote being the stimulus which drives the politician. In each case the karateka and politician are seeking stimulation which can only be realized upon the proper response.

The Karate Consciousness

A third type of learning theory is gestalt-field psychology in which there exists the development of insight and utilization of "feelings" and intuitions to solve problems.

Gestalt-field theorist counter that the S-R associationists err in making synonymous the observable results of learning and the learning itself. They argue that a change in physiological behavior does not necessarily mean that learning has occurred. A person who is struck from behind and knocked down may gain from this experience a healthy respect for dark alleys, but the change in behavior – falling down – is not equivalent to a change in insight. Furthermore, a person may use insights he has had for some time as a basis for change in his present behavior (Learning Theories for Teachers, Morris L. Bigge, Harper & Row Publishers, New York, 1964, pp. 96-109).

Obviously, there are differences of opinion regarding learning theory even among experts. Yet, this does not obviate the teacher of karate from familiarizing himself with knowledge of this kind. It is all valuable for student edification and learning.

In addition to learning theory the teacher should have an understanding of learning and teaching levels. "Rote-memorization" is the most basic but, perhaps, the least effective in generating thought and developing mental faculties. It is necessary in many cases, such as the memorization of tables, mathematical and scientific data, literary passages, etc., but it does relatively little to enhance the thinking process.

Richard Andrew King

A second learning level would be "understanding" which . . .

Seeks to acquaint students with the relationship between a generalization and the particulars – between principles and solitary facts – and which shows the uses to which the principles may be applied (Ibid. p. 323).

A third level, "reflective," makes use of all the principles of the previous level in addition to having the student become more actively involved in examining and testing the concepts he has learned. Therefore, there is a considerable amount of independent thinking with emphasis on the scientific approach. It is this level which engenders the most problem-solving capability. It makes the student think, not just regurgitate. Thus, it is the highest level of teaching and obviously the one which should be considered the most favorable by the teacher (Ibid. pp. 315-350). After all, the goal of all good teaching is not to create robots but vital, active, expanding, intelligent and lucid minds which can increase individual vibration and eventually effectuate transition to the next level of existence.

Aside from learning theories and teaching levels, the karate instructor should also give consideration to social, economic, religious and cultural influences. Not everyone can be taught in the same manner. Quite the contrary.

For instance, different races and cultures have varying experiences and viewpoints of life. As the teacher is aware of this, he can use different methods of instruction appropriate for each group.

The Karate Consciousness

And, of course, each individual, regardless of cultural ties, is different from everyone else. This is where teaching becomes interesting. Such a variety of individuals always creates challenges and forces the instructor to think and act in various ways in order to effectively convey the subject matter to be taught.

Also to be considered is the type of relationship the teacher desires to establish with the students: authoritarian, laissez-faire or democratic?

An authoritarian teacher exercises firm, centralized control. He closely directs every action of his students. He does all the planning for the class and issues all the directions. Furthermore, he tells students what to think as well as what to do. In an authoritarian classroom a teacher regards himself as the sole active agent and considers students passive receivers of instruction and information. Consequently, an authoritarian teacher is most likely to adhere to a mental disciplinary, apperceptive or S-R associationistic theory of learning (Ibid. p. 313).

The laisses-faire teacher goes to the opposite extreme. Since, by his actions, he commits himself to a psychology of natural unfoldment, he does not really lead at all. He is present, he may answer questions, but essentially he leaves students 'on their own.' Students decide what they want to do and how they will do it (Ibid. pp. 313-314).

Richard Andrew King

The democratic teacher . . . *plays the role of a democratic group leader. His chief purpose is to lead his students in the significant problems in the area in which he is teaching. Such study presupposes interchange of evidence and insights, give and take, and respect for one another's ideas. In a democratic classroom the teacher's ideas are subject to criticism just as are those of students. Although the teacher may be an authority on his subject, and to teach best should be, the situation is arranged so that students are encouraged to think for themselves* (Ibid. p. 314).

In the teaching of karate today it is a fair assumption that little work is being undertaken by instructors in view of the aforementioned teacher-student relationships. Without a doubt, the most prevalent type of karate instructor is, "authoritarian."

What must be considered, however, by every instructor of the art is student unfoldment and growth. An authoritarian approach may be justified in the incipient stages of a karateka's development because a whole new set of bodily positions, movements and exercises must be learned correctly. Also, control has to be developed to an appropriate level, and responsibility for utilizing the various strikes, blows and blocks engendered. But beyond the intermediate stage of development the instructor should begin diluting the authoritarian methodology and transfer emphasis to another type.

Students need to learn to think for themselves, if they haven't already. If they're always told what to think, such instruction will

The Karate Consciousness

not serve them well in life. Each person is unique, and any attempt to blanket or suppress his individuality is hazardous to his well-being. Therefore, to always teach in an authoritarian manner is highly questionable. It may be easy for the teacher but unhealthy for the student.

Another consideration regarding this matter is that the authoritarian teacher is precluding his own professional growth. If he tries nothing else, nor seeks to engender higher principles of life in his teaching methodology such as freedom, individuality, creativity and so forth, he can become nothing else, and the process of continually "becoming" is an unequivocal necessity in a universe of change. To be better, the teacher must initiate actions to make himself so.

It is for this reason that the karate instructor should learn and apply other alternatives of the student-teacher relationship. The laissez-faire approach may be justifiable in some cases. However, not having any control of the situation is just as questionable as being completely authoritarian. In the pursuit of self-esteem, students need to have some degree of direction, discipline and guidance. This is especially true for the more precocious individuals.

This brings us to the "democratic" type of relationship in which the teacher is a leader, one who shows the way but allows for and, in fact, promotes the faculty of individual thought. This approach may be considered the middle ground between authoritarian and laissez-faire.

Richard Andrew King

The democratic teacher is not overly concerned with his position being undermined as, for instance, an authoritarian teacher would be. This is because he's not concerned with a power position in the flock. His power flows from within; it is an inherent and intrinsic part of his Being, as it is in all people, and nothing can ever undermine or jeopardize it. He is free and unafraid and can, therefore, teach with pronounced fluidity and aplomb.

The student, of course, benefits by such a state of affairs. His learning environment is free, and he can express his own ideas, even question those presented to him if necessary, without fear of being suppressed or chastised. In all, he can grow and think or, at least, have the opportunity to do so. His well-being is, thus, enhanced and promoted.

This type of teacher-student relationship obviously takes work, especially on the part of the instructor. It is not as easy as the authoritarian method but not as restrictive either. It is an atmosphere in which both the teacher and student can grow and learn for, after all, devoid of roles and labels, students and teachers are still people – living, breathing, growing, vital and beautiful expressions of the life force.

In summation, it would be helpful if teachers of karate focused some of their attention on professionalization. In this process of upgrading they will benefit, their students will benefit, and the mass consciousness will receive another boost in its own edification.

The Karate Consciousness

STUDENT EMPHASIS

What I am, all that I am, reflects itself
in the lives of the lives I teach.

A teacher, any teacher, is only as good as the functional demonstrability of any one of his students. If a teacher is an advocate of self-discipline, for example, his students should embody it in their actions. As a tree is known by its fruit, likewise a teacher is known by his students.

It is the student who is the focal point of the teacher. This does not mean that the latter has no identity in the absence of the former. He is still an individual, but rather, it suggests that in order for a teacher's life to have full meaning, he must have someone to teach, just as an actor must have an audience and a painter a canvass. It seems like a rather simple idea and, indeed, it is, but in practice it is, oftentimes, not so simple. Individuals will sometimes instruct people for other primary reasons than student enhancement – money and ego inflation to name two.

The preceding paragraph is attempting to say that a teacher must care for and be dedicated to the well-being, enrichment, enhancement, growth and edification of his students. People come to him to learn, and he must not violate their trust. It is his obligation to do all he can to insure their learning is productive.

Richard Andrew King

What the student learns is placed on the instructor's shoulders, and the latter should not approach this matter without a high degree of conscience. Every individual is a splendid and magnificent creation and, concomitantly, he is deserving of lessons which coincide with such attributes. The richness of life, its infinity, beauty, meaning, priceless value and vitality are all focal points of student learning. The lessons described heretofore on love, thought, individuality, integrity, purity, discipline, control, strength, priorities and possessions are mainstreams of concentration for the karateka.

Above all else, the teacher of karate must remember that the true meaning of life is realized in the expression of Divine Perfection, and it is his purpose to assist his students in the fulfillment of this expression. Karate is, indeed, an excellent tool for self-development and a beautiful art form, but in the final analysis it is the student and teacher who make it so.

Finally, if there is any thought which the student or teacher of karate can use to enhance his own development or to give greater meaning to the karate consciousness it is this:

> Let your hands give wings to your mind
> that you may find an ever-greater power of life,
> a power preserving the sanctity of your soul and
> illuminating the radiance of your perfection.

The Karate Consciousness

Chapter 12

KARMA

Karma. Who is there who has never heard the word, *karma*? Who is there who has never used the word *karma* flowing freely from the lips in common conversation? Who is there who truly understands what karma means? Who is there who actually *lives* by karmic law?

For the karateka and, in fact, for every student and artisan of life, karma cannot be ignored. It must be understood, embraced and solidly ensconced within the deepest recesses of each and every serious aspirant seeking an elevated consciousness. Being ignorant of the great Law of Karma will completely negate individual ascent.

Richard Andrew King

Is it not beyond the realm of fact to say that if people really understood karma they would not be doing what they're doing every second of every day of their lives? Is it not beyond the realm of fact to say that most of us simply give lip service to the idea of karma rather than following its precept? Is it also not accurate to say that karma is a philosophy lightly discussed but universally ignored by the masses?

What is karma? Saint Sawan Singh (19th/20th Century) proclaims:

> *The law of karma is the principal law of the creation:*
> *as the action, so is the reward.*

Saint Jagat Singh, a 20th Century mystic states:

> *The law of karma is universal. It is the fixed and*
> *immutable law of nature. Each soul must reap*
> *what it has sown. Every soul shall have to*
> *bear the exact consequences of its actions.*

He goes on to say:

> *The Law of Karma is a self-operating law of cause and*
> *effect. A seed sown must sprout. Whatever you sow now,*
> *you will have to reap either in this birth or the next.*
> *Every action produces reaction which in turn produces*
> *further reactions and this vicious circle goes on forever.*

The Karate Consciousness

The germane item of note regarding karma is that it is a law. It is not a frivolous concept, guideline or whim of imagination to be discarded as if it had no bearing on our lives or actions. Laws are not arbitrary. And although man's laws are capricious, malleable and changeable, natural laws, especially divine laws, are not. They are absolute, unchangeable, immutable, inexorable. As humans, we don't get to choose whether we're affected by them or not. And directly to the point – we don't get to choose whether we're affected by karmic law or not. We are bound by it, bound to it, regardless of whether we're a king, queen, president, celebrity, pop star, commoner, pauper, man, woman or child. No one escapes karmic law, no one.

Yet, do we not go through life minute to minute, moment to moment, oblivious to the reality of the law of karma? It's as if we think we're special, that somehow we are not bound by our actions, our thoughts, our motives. It's almost as if we mock karmic law, which is a tragic flaw in us, is it not?

From the Bible, Galatians 6:7, we read:

> *Be not deceived; God is not mocked: for whatsoever*
> *a man soweth, that shall he also reap.*

Think of the power of this statement, deeply think about it, deeply. "For whatsoever a man soweth, that shall he also reap." This means that we will have to experience everything we do or say or think. We will not be able to escape the consequences of our thoughts and deeds. They will rebound to us in a heap of reaping in spite of any weeping we will endure.

REAPING WEEPING

© 1998 by Richard Andrew King
From *99 Poems of the Spirit*

Forever have we planted seeds –
the fetters of our keeping;
and now we find ourselves distraught,
distressed, and reaping weeping.

We close our eyes and shun the Law,
unconcerned of havoc wreaking;
and now, with storms upon us,
we cry unceasing, reaping weeping.

So immersed in petty selves
and in life's treasures we were stealing,
we never paused to ponder
that one day we'd be reaping weeping.

It's hard to feel sympathy
for those who spend defeating
the very purpose of this life
as they scream, reaping weeping.

The Karate Consciousness

We do have choices in this life,

and if it's Goodness we wish keeping,

then we should watch the seeds we're planting

or we'll be reaping weeping.

If we lie, cheat, steal, deceive, betray, adulterate, berate, hate, manipulate, love, support, encourage, nurture, purify – whatever it is we do, we will experience the exact same thing, inescapably.

Saint Jagat Singh declares:

Not even a single grain that inadvertently enters your granary from a neighbor's field can go unaccounted. You simply must pay for what you get. The law is inviolable and it cannot be set aside. The payment may be either in kind, in coin or by transfer of an equivalent good karma, but payment there must be.

Buddha affirms:

If you fear pain, if you dislike pain, don't do an evil deed in open or secret. If you're doing or will do an evil deed, you won't escape pain: it will catch you even as you run away.

Richard Andrew King

Saint Ravidas (15th/16th Centuries) echoes Buddha's statement with this offering:

The fruit of action unfailingly overtakes the doer.

Saint Dariya of Bihar (17th/18th Centuries) proclaims:

The sower of the poison cannot but be engulfed in the poison.

Saint Sawan Singh (19th/20th Centuries) reminds us:

The Karmic Law is inexorable and operates without regard to persons.

and . . .

The Karmic Law is supreme and inevitable and the sooner we reconcile ourselves with it the better.

Saint Charan Singh (20th Century) admonishes:

Karma – nobody can escape, whether one believes it or not.

Saint Dadu Dayal (16th Century) voices these thoughts:

What you have not done will never befall you. Only what you have done will befall you.

The Karate Consciousness

Saint Dadu further adds:

> *What has been done before appears now; what is done now will appear hereafter.*

And so it goes – from Saint to Saint, age to age, culture to culture – the truth of karma is always the same. It is not affected by monarchial edicts, presidential decrees, political correctness, group think, angry protestations or the endless changing of tides within the mercurial mind of man and mankind.

Truth is truth and truth never changes. That's why it's truth. The truth of karma is that whatever we put onto the circle of life will, without fail, circle back to encircle us eventually, at some time in some life. Therefore, if we're wise and sentient, we will not give lip service to anything we do or say but rather be ever mindful of what we sow – in thought, word and deed – because whatever we sow we shall reap. This is the law of this creation and it is inexorable, immutable, extant and eternal.

So how does the truth of karma manifest in our lives? Simple.
If we lie, we will be lied to.
If we kill, we will be killed.
If we love, we will be loved.
If we injure, we will be injured.
If we abort, we will be aborted.
If we cheat, we will be cheated.

Richard Andrew King

If we betray, we will be betrayed.

If we nurture, we will be nurtured.

If we steal, we will be stolen from.

If we support, we will be supported.

If we adulterate, we will be adulterated.

If we deceive others, we will be deceived.

Whatever we do will be done to us. This is the truth of karma, and no one escapes it. No one.

It cannot be more simple. What we do will be done to us at some future time. By karmic law it is impossible for the reaping not to follow the sowing. Thus, there is perfect justice in the world, regardless of thought to the contrary. Therefore, it would be extremely prudent for us to think and reflect on our actions before we execute them. If we want a good life, a happy life, an harmonious life, we must *live* karma, not give lip service to it.

For the karateka, Karmic Law takes on an especially critical element because martial arts can reap massive destruction, harm, even death to an individual. Therefore, as practitioners of this warrior art, if we unnecessarily and egotistically injure, harm, maim or even kill an individual through the misuse of our skills, we will suffer the same fate eventually. It is inescapable. Therefore, student of karate, beware! Violations of your art will result in you being violated. It is spiritually lawful to protect oneself from harm, but the willful injury or death of another beyond the boundaries of reason will bring identical consequences. As the sowing, will be the reaping. Be warned!

JUSTICE

© 1998 by Richard Andrew King
From *99 Poems of the Spirit*

Logic doesn't rule the world.
The Law of Karma does.
It is the way the world works
since the world was.

In counterpoint to justice lacking
in this world of women, men;
in Truth, there's total justice
from beginning to the end,

for Justice rules through karma,
not through human laws.
Justice is Divinely based;
its roots in Godly Cause.

Think not there is no justice.
There is, but we're confined
to understand its workings
from this side of the Blind.

Richard Andrew King

Remember, karma is inexorable.

Its justice is unflawed.

There never is injustice

in the Hallowed Halls of God.

*What you have not done will
never befall you.*

*Only what you have done will
befall you.*

~ Saint Dadu Dayal
(16th Century)

Chapter 13

CLIMBING THE
MOUNTAIN

There are three things to know about climbing the Mountain – the metaphor for divine ascent. First, it is never crowded on the top of the Mountain. Second, it is very difficult to climb the Mountain, which is why it is never crowded. Third, there is, as Saints and Mystics tell us, a secret doorway at the top of the Mountain leading to a secret passageway to the Inner Worlds, His World. If we can climb the Mountain, we have the opportunity to knock at that secret door and gain entrance to His Divine Reality. That is the promise of spiritual scripture.

Richard Andrew King

The Mountain is not a physical mountain but a spiritual mountain, the Mountain of Divine Consciousness which one ascends through concentration and a lifestyle commensurate with purification and perfection.

Returning to our first statement, it's never crowded on the Mountain. Why? Because most people are satisfied with living on the Valley Floor (the worldly consciousness) below at the base of the Mountain. The Mountain is there, always there, but few are they who challenge it. The Valley Floor is familiar, comfortable, secure, filled with people, things, activities, delights – you name it, it's there. It's also comfortable to be with lots of other people. Too, it is warmer and more inviting on the Valley Floor, and the effort of the climb up the Mountain simply involves too much stress, hardship and discomfort for comfort-driven souls.

The Mountain is severe. It's steep, slick, cold, uninviting, unfamiliar. Just its overwhelming austere presence is enough to frighten most people away. It takes a great deal of courage to even think of climbing the Mountain, not to mention the energy and time involved in its ascent. Furthermore, those who successfully climb it strangely never come back, which frightens most of the Valley Floor residents. Why go to all that trouble and endure the hardship of a dangerous and difficult climb and never be heard from again? Why leave one's friends, attachments, activities, comforts, securities and familiarities of the Valley Floor anyway? Doesn't make much sense, right?

The Karate Consciousness

Well, the reason a few people leave the comfort and security of the Valley Floor and make the arduous journey up the Mountain is because they have heard the rumors of the secret doorway leading to the secret passageway, leading to the Inner Worlds, leading to eternal freedom for the soul from the binding and incarcerating environment of the Valley Floor below, inclusive of its so called comforts and securities.

There is a mystical mystery about the Mountain which spiritually 'touched' souls cannot resist. Although few in number, they are the ones who climb. They are the ones who risk. They are the ones who leave the comfort, security and familiarity of the Valley Floor below to pursue a spiritual fascination. They are the ones who struggle, endure untold privations and hardships, and they are the ones who succeed in getting to the top of the Mountain and entering the secret door, leading to the secret passageway, leading to their ultimate spiritual freedom and soul liberation from the confines of this dimension.

THE CLIMB

Why does a person climb the Mountain? Because he feels a pull from It, an irresistible, compelling force – a magical, mystical, mysterious, marvelous magnetism that keeps drawing, ever drawing, his attention inward, upward, onward. Most of the time the pull is inexplicable. It is certainly invisible. It's just there,

Richard Andrew King

always there, tugging at the heartstrings of the soul, the conscience, the consciousness.

If one tries to pull away, the force pulls harder in return, always redirecting the focus of the attention to the Mountain, to its austerity, to its overpowering and omnipotent majesty and mystery. Helpless is the soul to avoid it. Helpless is the soul to explain it. Helpless is the soul to fight it. Helpless is the soul, helpless, and so it looks at the mountain with awe and longing, even fear and apprehension, but, still, it begins to climb, to ascend, to escape, to be free from the prison that is the Valley Floor below.

The soul begins its journey, its climb, irresistibly and helplessly, unknowing of what lies ahead. But it doesn't care. The compulsion is almost an insanity in itself. It is as if the soul were injected with some numinous nepenthe – a spiritual potion inducing the soul to forget and let go of its life on the Valley Floor and climb, climb into some unknown territory, some uncharted ground, holy ground, that will satisfy its eternal longing for eternal peace.

The soul soon learns that this is a solo climb. No holding hands here unless it is the Hand of God. No traveling buddies. No companions. No partners. The soul goes alone, ever pulled by the sweet magnetism of the mellifluous melodies within. Up it goes, step after step, falling, stumbling, sliding back a little but regaining its stability and composure and pressing on. It is a snail's pace this climb. Yet, with every micro inch of elevation gained, a whole new reality is gained, a whole new panorama, a whole new consciousness.

"If this is what is gained only after a tiny distance," asks the soul, "what will I experience if I climb some more?" And so the soul pushes on, ever on. It is addicted to the climb because the climb brings heretofore unknown perceptions and understandings it did not nor could have possessed while living on the Valley Floor below because it just wasn't high enough to see. Its vision was limited, extremely limited, as only its current experience can verify. In fact, the soul learns that, for all intents and purposes, it was, indeed, blind while living on the Valley Floor. It only knows this because now, because of its climb, because of its acquired elevation, it sees and sees clearly everything below it. But it doesn't see all because it has not ascended to the top of the Mountain, but it wants to see so it presses on . . . and on . . . and on – another step, another stumble, another slip, another slide but, yet, another reconviction to stay strong and press on.

SACRIFICE

It is not long into the journey up the Mountain that the soul learns this is a *sacrificial* climb. In other words, there are sacrifices, major sacrifices, to be made and sustained if one is to be successful in the ascent and reach the top of the Mountain, reach the secret door leading to the secret passageway, leading to the Inner Worlds. The soul learns that just as the greatest gift exacts the greatest price, so the greatest accomplishment exacts the greatest sacrifice.

Sacrifice means to surrender, to give up, to forego, to deny. By its very nature sacrifice, therefore, involves loss, but loss in exchange for something else. What is that loss? What is that 'something else'? For the spiritually driven soul, the loss is life within the Valley Floor. The 'something else' is eternal life within His Kingdom, the Kingdom of God, the Kingdom of the Creator.

Ravidas, a Saint of the 15th/16th Centuries exclaimed,

> *Let not my love for the Lord ever decrease.*
> *Dearly have I bought it in exchange for my life.*

Ravidas understood, and understood exceedingly well, the cost of climbing the Mountain. He gave up his life to seek His Life. He sacrificed his worldly life to gain eternal life with the Lord, with the Creator. This is the great accomplishment. But this accomplishment also, therefore, demands the greatest price and, in this case, it is the releasing, the sacrificing of one's worldly attachments.

Ravidas also stated:

> *For myriads of births have I been separated from*
> *Thee, O Lord. This birth is dedicated to Thee.*

The Karate Consciousness

Here Ravidas references the Law of Transmigration involving the reincarnation of his soul in a myriad of births in which he led his life in every which way but that of the Lord. However, in his sojourn as a wandering soul through countless lives, Ravidas finally came to understand there is no greater achievement than to live for the Lord, to climb the Mountain and Merge in Him, which is why he made the above statement of dedicating his life to God.

Every Mountain Climber must do the same thing – dedicate his life to the Lord, to the Power that created us, sustains us, graces us with life. Such dedication is the only way up the Mountain because, in reality, the Lord is the Mountain.

Does this mean one has to turn his back on the world? Well, yes. When we climb up a mountain, any mountain, is not our back turned toward the valley floor below? Is not our focus directed forward to each step in the climb? To go forward means we look forward and climb forward. If we were to look back, we would most definitely fall because we would not be able to see each and every foothold, every handhold, and we would, sooner or later, lose our step, our grip, and fall.

However, does climbing the Mountain mean we turn our back on our worldly duties and responsibilities? Absolutely not. Just the opposite. To climb the Mountain we do not run away to a mountain and become a recluse. The mystical and marvelous reality about the Climb is that the Mountain is within us; the Climb, therefore, is within us. We stay right where we are. The

Richard Andrew King

Mountain Climb is a climb in consciousness. It is not a physical climb. Therefore, we climb by purifying our consciousness while discharging our duties and responsibilities in the world to family, friends and occupation.

Furthermore, this discharging of our worldly duties and obligations is not sterile. It is an ever growing process which involves ever-increasing levels of being extremely loving, kind, warm, compassionate and heartfelt. The Climb, because it takes us 'higher', gives us higher values, higher principles, higher levels of understanding of love, life and light, all of which affect the way and manner in which we deal with the people, responsibilities and events in our personal lives.

MIS-READ & MIS-FOCUS

When the soul first feels the pangs of the pull from the Mountain, there is often the possibility of a mis-read and a subsequent mis-focus of the energy. The Mountain is pure spirit and, therefore, when we feel it, we also want to express that pure spirit. The mis-read is that we think we have to change the people, conditions and circumstances in the Valley Floor and that, somehow, if we can make it pure and good, all will be good, we will be good and happy. The Valley Floor will then be a wonderful place in which to live and we would have built a paradise on earth.

However, that is not the purpose of the pull. The pull is designed to pull each of us to a higher spiritual level individually, not collectively, nor change the environment of the Valley Floor. After all, every mountain needs its valley floor, has a valley floor. It's part of the divine design of creation. Without the valley floor, the mountain could not exist.

Furthermore, mystics tell us that the Valley Floor (the world) will always be the Valley Floor. It will never be paradise. That's precisely why mystics come to the Valley Floor – to take souls up the Mountain, to guide them Home to Paradise.

As Saint Charan Singh states:

We cannot reform this world, and this world will never become a heaven but will remain at daggers drawn, and there always will be killing in this world. Saints do not come to reform this world. They just come to take us away from this world.

If God wanted to change the Valley Floor or the conditions within it, or its inhabitants, He could do so in a nano flash. This is all God's creation and He does with it as He pleases. He is, after all, omnipotent. Every soul belongs to him, and He takes care of each soul as He thinks best.

The Valley Floor is not supposed to be changed because it is a proving ground for the soul, a furnace through which the soul is

Richard Andrew King

purified and cleansed before it makes its ascent. Not all souls ascend the Mountain at the same time. If they did, there would be no Valley Floor and this creation could not exist.

Therefore, when each of us feels the pull, our task is not to direct the energy outward in an attempt to change the Valley Floor but to direct our attention inward where the ascent occurs, i.e., within ourselves. Ironically, if we change for the positive, then the environment of the Valley Floor will also change for the positive to the degree of one soul better.

Besides, in consideration of changing the Valley Floor, how difficult a task is it? How hard is it to change ourselves, let alone change others or the entire Valley Floor? It's always easier to try to change others because it directs the focus of our cleansing and purification away from us and, of course, none of us needs purifying and cleansing, right?

Thus, if we mis-read the energy pull of the Mountain, we will naturally mis-focus, mis-direct our attention which must not be on others or the world of the Valley Floor, but on us, in us. The climb is a solo climb remember, and although it may be our time to climb, it may not be someone else's time to climb. Therefore, let us not mis-read the pull lest we mis-direct our focus, which is to get up the Mountain for ourselves. A mis-read and a subsequent mis-focus will only thwart our progress and ultimate success. When we finally make it up the Mountain, when we have the experience of getting to the top and discovering what waits for us there, then we can share with others what we've discovered, if they are amenable to listening.

CLIMBING STRESS

When we do begin our ascent of the Mountain, will there be stress in the climb? You bet! Tons of it! Don't be deceived. Expect it. Climbing is never an easy experience, especially over personally uncharted ground. Just as climbing a physical mountain is strenuous, so is climbing the spiritual Mountain, even more so.

When we ascend any mountain, we are always working against the pull of gravity which weights us down and forces us to work to climb higher. It's exhausting. When we climb the spiritual Mountain, we must work against the pull of the mass consciousness and its natural gravity. With every step we take, we will feel the downward pull. Thus, we must fight and work hard to ascend.

As we climb the Mountain, we will have to deal with the weight we carry on our own backs, the karmic load we've accumulated throughout our existence on the Valley Floor. We may also have issues with our own feelings, attitudes and beliefs. Attachments and desires of and possibly for the Valley Floor below may be concerns inhibiting our own focus as we climb. Memories of pleasant times below may crop up as the stress of the climb manifests itself in greater degrees. This may, likewise, tend to affect us negatively.

However, if we're meant to climb, we will. The upward pull will be stronger than its downward counterpart, and we will climb. The higher we climb, the more detached will the Valley Floor become until, because of our own height in the ascent, it will be virtually invisible below. It is just like being in an airplane. When it's on the ground, we can see everything on the ground. However, when it is in a higher altitude, people, activities and objects on the Valley Floor below become virtually non-existent to the eye. So it is with spiritual ascent. When we get high enough, we will become oblivious of that which is below and it will be of no concern to us. Out of sight, out of mind. Just as well.

It will, of course, take time and effort before we reach such a stage. Until we get there, we must endure the stress of the climb. It is a natural aspect of ascent, however unpleasant; but it must be endured. As muscles grow under the stress of physical weight training, so our spiritual muscles grow under the stress of spiritual training. As they become stronger, so do we, and we press forward with greater ease, skill and comfort.

Therefore, the message regarding the stress of the climb is that we must embrace it, accept it. It is a natural part of the process of ascent, and it will not go away. We just have to be disciplined and focused in our work, the work of climbing, of ascending, not descending.

The Karate Consciousness

THE ENIGMA

There is an enigma in climbing the Mountain and it is this: we have to climb it while residing within the Valley Floor. The climb, as we have said, is one of consciousness, not physicality. Therefore, we have to constantly be purifying our consciousness as we physically live and exist in the Valley Floor. On the outside, our physical appearance may not change. However, on the inside, appearances and realities will change drastically.

Climbing the Mountain creates a whole new reality which also changes with each step up the Mountain we make. Thus, our perceptions of the Valley Floor, its inhabitants, activities, environment, conditions, purpose, etc. etc., will also change – from the inside out. As our perceptions change, so will our understanding of life and its concomitant goals, drives and desires.

This enigma is why mystics tell us to live in the Valley Floor but not to become a part of it. In fact, the admonition is: just live in it but get out of it! This won't make much sense until we start climbing, and then it will make total sense . . . to us but not to others. In order to understand what it's like to be on the Mountain, one has to climb it. There is just no other way to understand. Experience is the best teacher, and when we get on the Mountain and involved with its ascent, we will then know what the Mountain holds and what the Mountain is; why it is difficult to conquer the Mountain and why, unmistakably why, it is such a

Richard Andrew King

critical necessity that we do so and do it now . . . while we still have the chance!

The thing for us to do is to get to the Light
ourselves as fast as possible.
~ Saint Sawan Singh

You do not belong to this world.
Just live in the world and get out of it.
~ Saint Charan Singh

INDEX

21st Century	122
Albert Einstein	84
Annie Besant	84
Anthony Norvell	83
Buddha	16, 84, 103, 227, 228
Climbing the Mountain, Ch. 13	233-246
Descartes	82
Divinology	196
Ed Parker	9
Extrinsic Power	26, 28-30, 32-33, 36-38, 40, 44, 94, 111
Futility Tunnels	199
Harold Keown	83
Helen Keller	170
Henrik Ibsen	42
Individuality, Ch. 6	125-140
Indomitable Calm	107, 163, 165
Intrinsic Power	26, 27, 28, 29, 32, 33, 34, 36, 44
Jesus	16, 103, 136
Kahlil Gibran	169
Karma, Ch.12	223-232
Kumite	30, 167
Love, Ch. 5	101-124
Mary Baker Eddy	83
Meanings, Ch. 1	9-24
Melvin Powers	83

Napoleon Hill	83
Plateaus	64
Power Precepts, Ch. 2	25-44
Priorities & Possessions, Ch. 10	191-206
Purity, Ch. 7	141-156
R. Eugene Nichols	84
Ralph Waldo Emerson	82
Saint Charan Singh	228, 241, 246
Saint Dadu Dayal	136, 228, 232
Saint Dariya of Bihar	136, 228
Saint Jagat Singh	13, 224, 227
Saint Ravidas	136, 228
Saint Sawan Singh	224, 228, 246
Second Millennium	122
Solomon	82
Strength, Ch. 9	179-190
Teaching, Ch. 11	207-222
The Continuum, Ch. 3	45-76
The D.C. Factor, Ch. 8	157-178
The Glass Lens	172
Thought, Ch. 4	77-100
Tracy Brothers	9
U.S. Anderson	83
Ulysses	76
Winston Churchill	169

The Karate Consciousness

RICHARD ANDREW KING
~ Books ~
RichardKing.net and Major Online Retailers

The Black Belt Book of Life
Secrets of a Martial Arts Master

The mystery and mystique of the martial arts is not only ages old, it's legend. Revered throughout the world, martial arts is a treasure chest of life secrets that transcend the boundaries of combat to include the expanse of life and living. Arguably, it is the greatest developmental system on earth for teaching the integration of body, mind and spirit

The Black Belt Book of Life: Secrets of a Martial Arts Master is not about physical fighting strategies and tactics. It is about concepts and principles we learn though martial arts training that can help us in the struggle of life, in the journey to conquer ourselves and gain the golden ring of our own completeness because in the end a true Black Belt should be a realized soul who, having engaged the enemy - himself - finds himself at the end of the journey, triumphant.

The Black Belt Book of Life: Secrets of a Martial Arts Master reveals many secrets of martial arts training, sharing these truths in quick and easy to read vignettes to benefit martial artists and the general public as well. It is a book for all readers, not just martial artists, both males and females, especially the youth of today who are in search of a foundation to guide their lives.

Richard Andrew King

Messages from the Masters
Timeless Truths for Spiritual Seekers

In a time where there is more need for enlightenment than ever before, *Messages from the Masters: Timeless Truths for Spiritual Seekers* offers timeless truths for genuine seekers thirsty for spiritual nectar. Masters are the PhDs of the universe, the Light Bearers of the Divine Flame. Their knowledge and wisdom are supreme. They have no equal. Although appearing human, they are not. Masters are the exalted Sons of God. Their chief duty is to rescue souls, liberating them from the maniacal maelstrom and madness of the material world and returning them to their eternal Home with the Lord.

Messages from the Masters is a rich source of hundreds of quotes from a cavalcade of nine Perfect Saints throughout the last six hundred years: Guru Ravidas, Kabir, Guru Nanak, Tulsi Sahib, Swami Ji Maharaj, Baba Jaimal Singh, Sawan Singh, Jagat Singh and Charan Singh. The messages in this book focus on the importance of the Divine Diet, the priceless Human Form, Reincarnation, the World, the Negative Power and Soul Food.

Warning! *Messages from the Masters* is not for the faint of heart or the worldly-minded. Masters come into the world to sever our attachment to it, not make it a paradise. Although the epitome of love and wisdom, they shoot straight from the hip, pull no punches, favor no religion. Their universal message of soul liberation is reflected in the statement of Saint Maharaj Charan Singh: *Just live in the creation and get out of it*!

99 Poems of the Spirit

99 Poems of the Spirit draws from the writings of Perfect Saints, Masters, Mystics and Sacred Scriptures. Designed to lift the consciousness, mind and heart, all of the poems are original works by Richard Andrew King. Their purpose is to help connect the reader with the mystic side of life in order to enhance the process of self-realization while advancing on the spiritual path and climbing the ladder leading to the ultimate attainment of God Realization. It is a treasure chest of poetic spiritual gems offered to excite, educate and stimulate the mind and soul in the glorious journey of spiritual ascent.

The Karate Consciousness

The Galactic Transcripts
TheGalacticTranscripts.com

The Galactic Transcripts will take you on a journey that is as provocative as it is mysterious. Its thirty-seven transmissions are channeled from a non-earth, alien group who identify themselves as members of the Space Brotherhood.

The Galactic Transcripts offer us descriptions of other worlds, their inhabitants, morals, ethics, and histories. They even forewarn of the coming cleansing of earth and the cataclysms preceding it. Other messages shed light on the original colonization of earth, telepathic communication, the power of love, the program of the Radiant One, and much more.

Those who have read *The Galactic Transcripts* have found them to be life-altering, profound, inspirational, transformative. Will they have that effect on you? Open your mind and allow the transcripts to take you beyond the limitations of our world and into new, undiscovered worlds far beyond our galaxy.

Destinies of the Rich & Famous
The Secret Numbers of Extraordinary Lives

Why are rich and famous people rich and famous? Is it luck? Hard work? Advantage by family name? What makes them special? What secrets are the basis of their success?

Destinies of the Rich & Famous explores the secret numbers of the following famous global icons and explains through The King's Numerology™ why they are both rich and famous - Dr. Albert Einstein, Amelia Earhart, Elvis Presley, General George Patton, Howard Hughes, John F. Kennedy, Marilyn Monroe, Michael Jackson, Muhammad Ali, Oprah Winfrey, Princess Diana and Sarah Palin

Destinies of the Rich & Famous answers these questions and much more. Too, it reveals the clear correlation between a person's life and his or her natal data - the date of birth and full name of birth, illustrating the reality that fame and fortune and destined!

Richard Andrew King

Blueprint of a Princess
Diana Frances Spencer - Queen of Hearts

The tragic death of Princess Diana of Wales - the most famous, the most photographed, the most written about woman of the modern world and possibly of all time - was one of the most shocking and saddening events of the late Twentieth Century. Not since the assassination of American President John Fitzgerald Kennedy in 1963, has such an event captured the attention of the world. On that ill-fated Sunday of 31 August 1997, and the following week until her funeral, there was much discussion and reflection of the Queen of Hearts, the People's Princess, England's Rose. But in all of the media news coverage, there was no discussion given to the cosmic aspects of her life and death.

Blueprint of a Princess is dedicated to addressing those issues through The King's Numerology^{tm}. Its purpose and hope is to offer some consolation and explanation as to that one question so poignantly written on a card of condolence left with the multitude of flowers before the gates of Buckingham Palace. . . "Why?"

After learning from King's teaching, it is impossible to conceive of going back to that 'twilight naive and foggy' state of being where one can only guess or hint at the truths, motivations and directions of one's life that are Pre-King. Not only do I recommend this book, but I suggest it and his other numerology books as absolutely necessary for the library of anyone even remotely interested in the science of numerology. ~ Hunter Stowers

The King's Book of Numerology
Volume 1-Foundations & Fundamentals

The King's Book of Numerology, Volume 1-Foundations & Fundamentals provides complete descriptions of Basic Numbers, Double Numbers, Purifier Numbers, Master Numbers, the Letters in Simple and Specific form as well as the Basic Matrix, the numerological blueprint of our lives.

"*The King's Book of Numerology* series contains new information that informs and predicts more completely and accurately than any previously published numerological work. It brings back the empowered sciences of long ago, information long since lost upon this plane." ~ G. Shaver

"The best numerology book I've ever read." ~ M.W.

The King's Book of Numerology II
Forecasting – Part 1

The King's Book of Numerology II: Forecasting – Part 1 is dedicated to opening the door to the divine blueprint of our lives. That plan, that divine blueprint of destiny, is exact, precise, unchangeable, unalterable and . . . knowable, at least in general terms.

Once this awareness of a predetermined fate becomes established through application of numbers and their truths, our understanding and consciousness of life will, no doubt, change. We will begin to see ourselves as part of an immense spiritual super-structure far beyond our current ability to comprehend, understand or perceive. Life will take on new meaning and, perhaps, we will even begin to awaken to greater spiritual truths. Subjects covered: Life Cycle Patterns, The Pinnacle/Challenge Matrix, Epoch Timeline, Voids, Case Studies and much more.

Richard Andrew King

The King's Book of Numerology 3
Master Numbers

The King's Book of Numerology 3 – Master Numbers delves deeply into the subject of master numbers – multiple digit numbers of the same cipher, focusing especially on binary master numbers: 11-22-33-44-55-66-77-88-99.

Master numbers are the nuclear component of the numeric spectrum and play powerful roles in the destinies of individuals. They cannot be ignored.

KBN3 reveals the process of discovering hidden master numbers in all facets of a King's Numerology^{tm} chart, how voids effect the life and much more.

The King's Book of Numerology 4
Intermediate Principles

The King's Book of Numerology 4 – Intermediate Principles will expand your consciousness of the mysteries of life and destiny by taking you deeper into the secret world of numbers and their meaning.

Life is energy. People are energy. Numbers are arithmetic codes describing and defining the energies that comprise our lives and destinies. Like priceless treasures discovered during an archaeological dig, numbers and number patterns buried beneath the surface of single numbers contain a treasure trove of untold wealth and secret riches of knowledge and wisdom.

Intermediate Principles chapters include Common Names, Linkage, Stacking, Name Suffixes, Binary Capsets, Influence/Reality Set Formats, Dual Basic Matrix Components, Subcap Challenges, and much more.

The King's Book of Numerology 5
I/R Sets – Level 1

IR SETS are the crux, core and substance of numerology forecasting, indispensable to the King's Numerology^{tm} system and to anyone choosing to know where they've been, where they are now and where they're headed. They are obligatory for any serious and professional numerologist.

The King's Book of Numerology 5: I/R Sets – Level 1 offers a general explanation of each of the 81 IR Sets in order to create a foundation on which to build a greater understanding of how life's events affect us. KBN5 is a starting point from which to grow greater knowledge of one's self and destiny.

IR SETS are a gift for those willing to receive them, study them and apply their vast level of knowledge to make our lives more understandable, manageable, easier, better, whole.

The King's Book of Numerology 6
Love Relationships

Note: This is a "stand alone" book. Its knowledge is not dependent on

prior KBN publications.

The *King's Book of Numerology, Volume 6 – Love Relationships* (KBN6) guides you through this revolutionary method of understanding the Secrets of Love and Happiness via the mystical science of numbers. If you can add 1 + 1, you can quickly learn how to utilize and benefit from the great truths shared within this book.

KBN6 is divided into two parts: Part 1 is the original book *Your Love Numbers*; Part 2 puts the King's Numerology^{tm} number science to the test with twenty marital case studies broken into three segments: Section I. Marriages rated as excellent; Section II. Celebrity marriages ending in divorce; and Section III. Hollywood marriages that have endured. These case studies are powerfully insightful because they reveal, without question, the dramatic and irrefutable correlation between love and numbers.

Richard Andrew King

The King's Book of Numerology 7
Parenting Wisdom

The King's Book of Numerology, Volume 7: Parenting Wisdom – Numerology & Life Truths (KBN7) is a compilation of two books in one. The reason for this is twofold: 1. To place the *Parenting Wisdom* series in one convenient resource; 2. As a continuing effort to place all King's Numerology[tm] books under one banner. KBN7 is also a "stand alone" book. Its knowledge is not dependent on having read prior KBN publications.

KBN7-Part 1: *Parenting Wisdom for the 21st Century – Raising Your Children by Their Numbers to Achieve Their Highest Potential* reveals the secrets to understanding a child's Basic Matrix and destiny through the most ancient of all sciences, numbers. Using numerology to help raise children is a revolutionary idea, reaping great rewards for children in helping them understand themselves, their life's journey and destiny.

KBN7-Part 2: *Parenting Wisdom – What to Teach the Children* offers thirty-three time-tested universal principles of life which parents can use to create a strong foundation for their children, allowing them to develop into whole, fulfilled and substantive adults. These thirty-three fundamental concepts offer parents a road map and paradigm of what to teach the children.

The King's Book of Numerology 8
Forecasting, Part 2

The King's Book of Numerology, Volume 8 – Forecasting, Part 2 broadens and expands the knowledge of numerology forecasting into areas of greater depth and specificity, giving students and practitioners of this divine numeric science tools unknown heretofore, allowing them to rise to the zenith of understanding in decoding life and destiny, and once again proving that life is destined and that the blueprint of destiny is, indisputably, secretly hidden in our birth names and birth dates. Indeed, God did not drop us here without a plan or a way of knowing that plan if we so choose.

- Contents -

The X-Y Paradigm, Cycle of Nines, Timeline Transitions, Lifetime Monthly Timeline (LMT), Annual Cycle Patterns – Monthly Timelines, Monthly Cycle Patterns (MCPs), Life Changes and the Number 5, Master Filters, Master Amalgams, Crown Roots/Pillars, Addresses – Homes and Businesses, Numerology Forecasting – Step-by-Step Analysis, and the 2016 Presidential Election Series – Articles: 1 to 10

The Age of the Female
A Thousand Years of Yin

The Age of the Female: A Thousand Years of Yin highlights the profound and extraordinary ascent of the female in the modern world, placing her center stage in the global spotlight as presidents and leaders of nations, titans of industry, corporate executives, military generals, media magnets, doctors, lawyers and a whole host of other prestigious titles normally associated with the male. Why has her rise to prominence been so rapid, especially in consideration of historic time? Why also has there been an increased interest in other people's lives in our society, in competitive athletics, personal data collection and the exploration of space and other worlds? *The Age of the Female: A Thousand Years of Yin* answers these questions. It is an insightful and exciting read into these mysteries, offering compelling and irrefutable evidence through the ancient science and art of numerology that, indeed, the age of the female has arrived and the next thousand years belong, not to him, but to her.

Richard Andrew King

The Age of the Female II
Heroines of the Shift

The Age of the Female II: Heroines of the Shift continues the remarkable journey of the female's ascent in the modern world of the 2nd Millennium. This installment is a general read in five chapters honoring the accomplishments of women in categories of female firsts, female Nobel laureates, female athletes, female icons and female quotations.

The achievements of the women featured in The Age of the Female II: Heroines of the Shift are deserving of respect and admiration. Their lives, challenges and successes are motivational catalysts for every individual to be the best he or she can be and to honor the very essence of what it is to be human. *The Age of the Female II: Heroines of the Shift* is intended to be an inspiring and educational read for everyone, not just women but men, too, offering knowledge and insight of the depth, power and daring-do of women as their Yin energy rises upon the global stage in this millennium which destiny has irrefutably marked as the Age of the Female.

Your Love Numbers
Discovering the Secrets of Your Life, Loves and Relationships

Published also as Part 1 of KBN, Volume 6 – Love Relationships

Your Love Numbers reveals the secret formula defining all great relationships and how to assess the love potential of any relationship in a matter of minutes.

Your Love Numbers teaches you how to assess a relationship or potential relationship in minutes, saving you endless time, energy, effort and possible heartache in the end. By knowing ourselves and the people we love, our relationships will be potentially more rewarding, satisfying, productive, peaceful, lasting and loving . . . for everyone - our family, spouses, partners, children, friends.

Parenting Wisdom
Raising Your Children By Their Numbers
To Achieve Their Highest Potential
(Published also as Part 1 of KBN7 – Parenting Wisdom)

Parenting Wisdom for the 21st Century - Raising Your Children by Their Numbers to Achieve Their Highest Potential is a revolutionary addition to the process of arguably the most important job in the world, parenting.

The powerful information contained within this work will reveal the hidden desires driving your children, the paths they will follow in life, the roles they will give on the great life stage and much more – all designed to augment your parenting wisdom and support life's paramount parental purpose . . . to love the children and help them achieve their highest potential.

ParentingWisdom.net

Parenting Wisdom 2
What To Teach The Children
(Published as Part 2 of KBN7-Parenting Wisdom)

This work is a companion book to *Parenting Wisdom For The 21st Century – Raising Your Children By Their Numbers To Achieve Their Highest Potential.*

Parenting is the most important and critical job in life because it encompasses the cultivating and sculpting of life itself as reflected in our children – the sanctity of life in manifest form.

In the process of parenting one of the most germane questions is, "What do we teach the children?" Parenting Wisdom offers thirty-three time-tested, universal principles which parents can use to create a strong foundation allowing children to develop into whole, fulfilled, and substantive adults.

ParentingWisdom.net

Richard Andrew King

The Karate Consciousness

RICHARD ANDREW KING
~ CDs ~
RichardKing.net, CDBaby.com, and Online Retailers

Priceless Poetry & Prose 1
Dramatizations of Famous Literary Works

Wonderfully entertaining and educational artistic dramatizations of famous literary works for adults, children, teachers and students alike. Enjoy the timeless words of Shakespeare, Lincoln, Tennyson, Longfellow, Patrick Henry, Emily Dickinson, Chaucer and more.

Priceless Poetry & Prose 2
Selected Works of Edgar Allan Poe

Be enveloped in the mysterious and haunted world of one of America's most loved poets, Edgar Allan Poe. Highly entertaining and educational, enjoy classic poems such as, The Raven, Annabel Lee, Ulalume, Alone, Lenore and more.

Poems of the Spirit
Selected Original Poems of Richard Andrew King

A collection of original spiritual poems designed to edify the mind and uplift the spirit. Not for the faint of heart or worldly-minded, these works reflect timeless truths from scriptures, saints and mystics throughout the ages - messages enabling the individual to break the shackles of worldly ties in quest for spiritual realization.

Echoes from the Heart
Selected Original Songs of Richard Andrew King

An original collection of twelve of Richard's tug-at-your-heart ballads, cowboy songs, patriotic tributes and spiritual tunes for your soul. A few titles are *Waiting for You*, *Don't Forget the Heroes*, *One More Broken Heart*, *The Promise*, *Rodeo Cowboy*, *You Can't Push the River*, *No Itty Bitty Cowboy* and *Catch Me When I Fall*.

Richard Andrew King

The Karate Consciousness

To order Books and CDs, go to

RichardKing.Net

or major online retailers

CONTACT

Richard Andrew King

PO Box 3621

Laguna Hills, CA 92654

RichardKing.Net

Rich @ RichardKing.net

Notes:

Notes:

Notes:

Notes:

The Karate Consciousness

www.ingramcontent.com/pod-product-compliance
Lightning Source LLC
Chambersburg PA
CBHW060012100426
42740CB00010B/1466